INVESTING IN FINANCIALLY DISTRESSED FIRMS

Investing in Financially Distressed Firms

A GUIDE TO PRE- AND POST-BANKRUPTCY OPPORTUNITIES

Murali Ramaswami
and
Susan E. Moeller

Q

QUORUM BOOKS
New York
Westport, Connecticut
London

Library of Congress Cataloging-in-Publication Data

Ramaswami, Murali.
    Investing in financially distressed firms : a guide to pre- and
post-bankruptcy opportunities / Murali Ramaswami and Susan E.
Moeller.
        p. cm.
    Includes bibliographical references.
    ISBN 0-89930-404-4 (lib. bdg. : alk. paper)
    1. Leveraged buyouts.   2. Leveraged buyouts—Case studies.
3. Bankruptcy.   I. Moeller, Susan E.   II. Title.
HD2746.5.R36   1990
332.6'722—dc20   89-10749

British Library Cataloguing in Publication Data is available.

Library of Congress Catalog Card Number: 89-10749
ISBN: 0-89930-404-4

First published in 1990 by Quorum Books

Greenwood Press, Inc.
88 Post Road West, Westport, Connecticut 06881

Printed in the United States of America

The paper used in this book complies with the
Permanent Paper Standard issued by the National
Information Standards Organization (Z39.48-1984).

10 9 8 7 6 5 4 3 2 1

Copyright Acknowledgments

The authors and publisher gratefully acknowledge permission to use the following copyrighted materials:

Excerpts from *Pensions & Investment Age*. Reprinted with permission, *Pensions & Investment Age*, March 6, 1989. Copyright Crain Communications, Inc.

Excerpts from "MCorp Under Siege." An R. D. Smith & Company Report, by Craig Davis and Randall Wooster, December 15, 1988.

Excerpts from *Managerial Finance*, Eighth Edition, by J. Fred Weston and Thomas E. Copeland, copyright © 1986 by The Dryden Press, a division of Holt, Rinehart and Winston, Inc., reprinted by permission of the publisher.

Excerpts from *Investment Perspectives*, "Message from the Spreads," by Byron R. Wien. Copyright 1989 Morgan Stanley Research.

Excerpts from "Stock Market Perception of Industrial Firm Bankruptcy," *The Financial Review* 22, no. 2 (May 1987) are used with permission.

Excerpts from Brian M. Doyle and Hoyt Ammidon III of Salomon Brothers Inc., "The Anatomy of a Leveraged Buyout," copyright © 1988 by Salomon Brothers Inc.

Excerpts from Paul H. Ross, Vincent J. Palermo, Varkki P. Chacko, and Peter M. Warlick of Salomon Brothers Inc., "High-Yield Corporate Bonds: An Asset Class for the Allocation Decision," copyright © 1989 by Salomon Brothers Inc.

Excerpts from Susan E. Moeller, "Chapter 11 Filings: Good News for Investors?" *AAII Journal*, April 1986, are used with permission.

To my parents, my wife Shoba,
and my son Vikas,
who, in their own unique ways,
contributed to the
completion of this book.

Murali Ramaswami

Contents

Illustrations

TABLES

FIGURES

Preface

The "overleveraging" of corporate America has emerged as one of the important socioeconomic and political issues of the 1980s. It has engaged the imagination of both the popular press and the serious academic thinker. Have the captains of industry suddenly become fiscally irresponsible? Is the latent greed of Wall Street and top corporate management surfacing through the endless succession of spectacular leveraged deals, as some sociologists suggest? Do the inevitable corporate restructuring and the consequent uprooting of established communities that follow a leveraged change of ownership cry out for a political solution? These are yet unresolved issues of the 1980s. What is clear, however, is that these leveraged companies are a fact of life and the investor has to recognize them as such.

Some of the pertinent questions that arise from the investor's perspective relate to the high risks that go with the high returns expected from investing in the securities of these firms. Integrated Resources, a major marketer of financial products including real estate limited partnerships, was one of Drexel Burnham Lambert's (the investment firm that created the huge junk bond market) junk-bond success stories until recently. In June 1989, Integrated defaulted on its junk IOUs (short-term, unsecured commercial papers). There are other examples in the book of leveraged companies that are now cash strapped and prone to default on their junk debt. Are these firms more prone to bankruptcy than the so-called blue chip companies? If they go bankrupt are their prospects for reorganization better than the bankrupt companies of yesteryears? Rules and the analytical framework adopted for investing in financially distressed firms are therefore relevant in this context. Some related issues considered in this book are: Are bankrupt firms better investments now that well-known firms like Texaco, Manville, and Eastern file for bankruptcy for reasons other than financial distress? Have investments in bankrupt firms been traditionally profitable investments? Are stocks or bonds of bankrupt firms better investments? Do stock prices signal the impending bankruptcy of a firm? Can bankruptcy be predicted using generally available accounting information? Have the new bankruptcy laws (Chapter 11 of the Bankruptcy Code) subtly encouraged and made it easy to file for bankruptcy? What are the laws that govern filing for bankruptcy and the subsequent reorganization or liquidation of the firm? Given that investing in a bankrupt firm that ultimately reorganizes can offer significant returns, are there ways to estimate the probability of reorganization? These are important questions for the investment manager and the financial institutions that participate in the sizable $200 billion high-yield debt market and funds that specialize in the investment of securities of financially distressed firms.

For the student of corporate finance, a study of the firms that are poised on the brink of bankruptcy (financially distressed firms) and the subsequent reemergence from bankruptcy offers a unique perspective of the increasingly leveraged (high-risk) environment of corporate America. We can all hope that the lessons learned from past failures can be employed to prevent future ones. The case studies given at the end of the book make it ideal for use in an MBA class on special topics in corporate finance. This book could also be used as a supplementary reading in the honors undergraduate seminar. The Ph.D student in search of interesting, unresolved issues requiring further investigation in the areas of corporate finance or investment management could use this book to generate dissertation topics.

This book consolidates for investors much of the available information on the nature of bankrupt securities and how to invest in them. The book is written for professional investors and students of corporate finance/investment management interested in some of the research that has been done in the area. It is our contention that the equities and bonds of bankrupt firms can be a good investment, and that an investor can earn returns that more than compensate for the risks taken. The increasing realization of this fact has eroded some of the potential returns, according to some in the investment management community. Many real-world examples are illustrated and some actual bankruptcy cases are presented. We also contend that a study of financially distressed firms with an objective to invest offers the appropriate framework of analysis to understand the burgeoning high-yield (junk bonds) market. The need to perform close credit analysis of securities with inadequate public information offers the parallel with the bankruptcy market. A brief description of the chapters follow.

Chapter 1 of the book introduces the concept of bankruptcy to the reader. During the 1980s more firms have filed for bankruptcy than during the depression years of the 1930s. The popularity of investing in bankrupt firms has increased along with their numbers. The chapter ends with a discussion of how an investor can wisely choose the best investment from the bankrupt securities available.

Chapter 2 discusses why firms are forced into bankruptcy. Most bankrupt firms develop cash flow problems because of sales downturns. Managements often are forced to acquire too much debt, which results in more cash flow problems. The core of the business, however, may still be of value to investors. This chapter discusses the differences between stocks and bonds of bankrupt companies. Depending on the nature of the business, one security in one company will be a better investment than that of another company. The chapter ends with a research study which shows that the returns to stockholders of bankrupt firms may be higher than they should have expected for the risk of the investment.

Chapter 3 illustrates the financial distress process that bankrupt firms go through. This section is of value to an investor as he or she needs to understand the environment in which a bankrupt firm finds itself, and what happens to a firm that is under the protection of the bankruptcy court.

Chapter 4 extends the information provided investors in chapter 3 to include how reorganizations and liquidations are processed. This chapter describes the provisions of the Chapter 11 law and its administration by the courts.

Chapters 5 and 6 have a more academic orientation than the beginning chapters. Research has shown that if an investor can choose a bankrupt firm that successfully reorganizes, then the returns from such an investment will be the highest for the risk involved. A model for making such a selection is included in chapter 5.

Chapter 6 presents more theoretical findings on the relationship between bankrupt firms and the stock market and the economy. The ability of the stock market to impound information (and thus reveal it) concerning the future state of the economy and issues related to the predictive power of the stock market in anticipating impending bankruptcies are presented.

The book concludes with a chapter of case studies of bankrupt firms. Chapter 7 will allow an investor unfamiliar with bankrupt investments a look at some balance sheets and income statements of financially distressed firms. It provides some insights into the legal problems a bankrupt firm faces and how investors may be affected. The use of the bankruptcy act to address corporate problems unrelated to inadequate cash flows, such as product liability and a mismanaged takeover, is illustrated through the case studies of Manville Corporation and Texaco. The chapter also illustrates the application of the Zeta scoring system to evaluate the probability of bankruptcy. Finally it shows some results of how shareholders would have fared if they had purchased the stocks of a bankrupt firm when the firm filed for Chapter 11 and if the stocks were held until reorganization occurred.

The authors hope that the reader of this book will find its information helpful in making sound investment decisions about bankrupt securities. Yet another purpose is served should the book facilitate further research by students of corporate finance/investment management.

We would like to express our debt to the College of Business Administration, Northeastern University, where part of the research presented in this book was conducted. We wish to acknowledge the persistent efforts of the acquisition editor, Liliane Miller, in keeping this project alive and the meticulous editing of our copyeditor, Katie Chase. We believe the book is the better for their efforts. All remaining errors, of course, are our responsibility.

Glossary

Absolute priority   A rule observed in a Chapter 7 and an old Chapter X bankruptcy proceeding under which net proceeds of liquidation or valuation of a failed firm's assets must be distributed. Each superior claim must be fully satisfied before the claim under it can receive anything.

Arbitrage   The simultaneous sale of one financial instrument and purchase of another that is exchangeable for the first. Arbitrage by traders tends to equate the market value of the exchangeable instruments.

Assets   Anything of value that is owned by some party. On the balance sheet of a firm, the assets are what the firm owns, such as cash, accounts receivable, inventories, land, buildings, and equipment.

Assignment   Transfer of the assets of a failed firm to an assignee or trustee, who takes over the management and either liquidates the assets or attempts to rehabilitate the firm.

Bankruptcy   A legal term indicating that a firm has been admitted to a proceeding under the Bankruptcy Reform Act of 1978, its assets are under the control of the bankruptcy court, and it will be either liquidated or reorganized.

Bankruptcy costs   Costs related to the probability that a firm may not be able to meet its financial obligations. These costs will rise at an increasing rate as the proportion of debt in the capital structure increases.

Bear market   When stock market players have expectations that the prices of stocks will decline.

Blue chip   A term used to describe the stocks of large stable companies. Buying such stocks is usually perceived by investors as a low-risk investment.

Book value   The value at which an asset, liability, or equity is carried on the firm's balance sheet. Book value per share of common stock is the total of the common equity accounts, common stock, additional paid-in capital, and retained earnings, divided by the number of shares outstanding.

Bull market   When stock market players have expectations that the prices of stocks will increase.

Call option   A contract that gives the holder the right to buy a stated number of shares of a given stock at a stated striking price any time on or before a given date. The writer of the option guarantees to sell the shares at the striking price if the option is exercised.

Capital asset pricing model (CAPM)   A model under which the required rate of return on an asset is estimated as a function of the risk-free rate, the required rate of return on the market portfolio, and the beta coefficient.

Capital gain   A gain from the sale of an asset at a price greater than its original cost.

Capital market   A financial market dealing in long-term equity securities.

Capital structure   The long-term and permanent financing of the firm.

Chapter 7 bankruptcy   A federal bankruptcy proceeding in which the assets of the firm are liquidated and the net proceeds are distributed to the firm's creditors in order of their priorities.

Chapter 11 bankruptcy   A federal bankruptcy proceeding in which the firm is reorganized under court supervision and the securities of the succeeding firm are distributed on an equitable basis to the claimants.

Common stock   The security held by the residual owners of a corporation.

Common stock equity   The net worth of the firm, less preferred stock, if any.

Composition   A settlement under which the creditors of a firm that cannot meet its obligations agree to accept a uniform percentage payment and absolve the debtor of the remaining debt.

Convertible bond   A bond that may, at the option of its owner, be exchanged for a predetermined number of shares of common stock.

Covered option   An option for which the writer holds the stock that is guaranteed to be delivered if the option is exercised.

Crown jewel strategy   A strategy to discourage a hostile takeover attempt under which the target firm's management announces a plan to sell the firm's most valuable assets to its current shareholders if the takeover attempt persists.

Current assets   Assets expected to be converted to cash within one year in the normal course of business.

Current liabilities   Amounts owed to a firm's creditors that are due within one year.

Current ratio   A ratio calculated by dividing the total current assets by total current liabilities.

Debentures   Bonds that are not secured by the pledge of specific property.

Debt ratios   Financial ratios that relate total debt to either assets or equity capital. Debt ratios provide measures of solvency.

Defaulted bonds   Bonds of companies that are in financial distress and can no longer pay interest payments.

Diversifiable risk   The risk that relates to a specific asset but can be offset by combining a number of assets into a diversified portfolio.

Diversification   Balancing defensively by dividing investments among a number of different assets subject to differing risk.

Dun & Bradstreet, Inc.   The largest mercantile credit reporting agency.

Economic failure   The inability of a firm to generate sufficient revenues to cover its costs, including the cost of capital.

Efficient market   A market in which prices adjust quickly and objectively to information about risk and returns of various securities.

Efficient portfolio   A portfolio of investments that provides the highest possible rate of return for a given level risk or the minimum risk for a given rate of return.

Equilibrium value   The market value of an asset when its market is in equilibrium.

Equity capital   Long-term or permanent capital invested in the firm by or on behalf of its owners.

Event risk   The risk that a restructuring of assets imposes on a firm.

Ex post return   The historical return on a security.

Extension   An informal arrangement under which the creditors of a firm that cannot meet its financial obligations agree to a postponement of maturity of debt obligations.

Fallen angels   Investment-grade bonds that have become junk or defaulted bonds.

Fixed assets   Assets of a relatively long-term or permanent nature, such as land, buildings, and equipment.

Going-concern value   The theoretical value of the common stock of a firm that is expected to continue in operation indefinitely.

Illiquidity   The financial state of a firm that is unable to meet its financial obligations as they become due. It is also called technical insolvency.

Income statement   The dynamic financial statement, disclosing the sales, costs and expenses, and profits made by a firm over a period of time, as determined by the accrual accounting process.

Insolvency   The financial state in which the liabilities of a firm exceed the real value of its assets; sometimes called absolute insolvency.

Junk bond   A high-yield high-risk bond usually used to finance leveraged buyouts.

Leverage   In finance the term is used to describe how the use of debt magnifies a firm's profits and losses when compared to a firm that is financed by equity alone.

Leveraged buyout (LBO)   A purchase of a company's stock with borrowed money, with the borrowings secured by the assets of the firm being acquired. Often a leveraged buyout is consummated by managers of the firm or a small group of investors.

Liquidation   The process of turning assets into cash.

Liquidation value   The net price at which an asset can be sold.

Liquidity   The ability to pay financial obligations as they come due.

Long position   Actually owning an asset.

Market equilibrium   The state of a market when the forces of supply and demand are equal.

Market portfolio   A portfolio theoretically consisting of all the securities available in the market. A broadly based index, such as Standard & Poor's 500 Stock Composite Index, is used as a proxy for the common stock market portfolio.

Market return   The rate of return on the market portfolio.

Market risk   The risk that affects all assets, but each to a varying degree. Also called nondiversifiable risk because this type of risk can not be diversified away by combining assets into a portfolio.

Market value   As applied to common stock, the value at which the stock is traded in the secondary market.

Net worth   The book value of the equity of a firm.

Poison pill   An agreement under which the current shareholders can purchase additional shares of a corporation's stock at an extremely low price. This device may be used in an effort to fend off a hostile takeover attempt, as it dilutes the value and voting power of shares held by or tendered to the acquiring firm.

Put option   A contract that gives the holder the right to sell a stated number of shares of a given stock at a stated striking price any time on or before a given date.

Reorganization   Under a Chapter 11 bankruptcy filing a company's debts and assets are restructured such that the company can start over without owing creditors any back payments.

Reorganization risk   When a company is going through a Chapter 11 filing, investors in that firm take on the risk that the company will emerge from Chapter 11 and the investors will lose because of the way the firm is restructured.

Restructuring of assets   When a company enters financial distress it is because it cannot pay its creditors. The courts or management work to get the firm's creditors to agree to take less than is owed them either in the form of cash or new securities of the firm. When both sides finally agree on what is fair and equitable then the company's assets are said to be restructured. The company usually has less debt than before it failed.

Reverse split When a company is reorganized, shareholders often are asked to accept a reverse stock split in which they receive fewer shares in the reorganized firm than they held in the old firm. They may be asked, for example, to give up 25 old shares for 5 new ones.

Risk The degree of potential variability of outcomes from forecasted values. The term is usually used interchangeably with uncertainty.

Risk-free rate of return The rate of return that can be earned on an investment entailing no risk except that of inflation.

Risk-neutral An asset is said to be risk-neutral when it earns the correct amount of return that compensates investors for the risk inherent in the asset.

Risk of default The possibility that a borrower may not pay interest or principal in full.

Risk premium The return in addition to the risk-free rate that investors require for bearing the risk of holding an asset.

Security The term is used to denote a financial instrument such as a share of stock, a bond, or a note.

Short position When investors agree to sell a security they do not own on the speculation that the price will decline.

Zero-coupon bonds A bond that does not require any periodic interest payments, only the principal at maturity. Such bonds are issued at deep discounts to provide a competitive return to the investor in the form of price appreciation.

INVESTING IN FINANCIALLY DISTRESSED FIRMS

Introduction

Leveraged buyouts (LBOs; public firms that are taken private, financed largely through risky, high-yield debt or "junk bonds" and minimal equity) of the 1980s could lead to workout investing of the 1990s. Welcome to the somewhat esoteric world of the workout banker. Although workout investing is not aerobics, it does call for some fancy footwork. It is the art of profitably rehabilitating near-bankrupt firms through financial restructuring. Most of the redeemable firms are the LBOs of yesteryear that are now burdened by the mountainous debts undertaken at the time of the privatization. Much of this debt will become equity in the laborious process of workouts. By a conservative estimate, fund managers and financial boutiques raised $2.5 billion for workout investing in 1987 alone. In many Wall Street firms, bankruptcy units—the poor cousins of mergers and acquisitions—are being rechristened the more glamorous financial restructuring groups.

THE LEVERAGED CORPORATE WORLD OF THE 1980s

An interesting hypothesis is to view the "overleveraging" (or the assumption of increasing levels of debt) of the corporate balance sheets as a natural extension of the entrepreneurial explosion evidenced in the United States during the 1980s. Much of the investment in new ventures and growth companies is high-risk. A supplanting of low-risk with high-risk capital in staid companies is one mode of introducing entrepreneurship in these companies. The new owner-managers now have an incentive to bring forth superior effort, while the investors in high-risk debt could be expected to monitor their investments more closely. This may be a valid prescription for individual companies, but is there a fallacy of composition (a logic that may be sound at the unit or individual level but is fallacious when carried over to the aggregate) in this argument when applied to the entire corporate sector of the United States? It depends.

It could be argued that the U.S. corporate sector could no longer afford the low debt/equity ratios of the 1950s and 1960s—the golden era for U.S. industry. The more competitive, globalized market environment of the 1980s and beyond calls for a greater measure of risk-taking by U.S. managers. Increasing the debt/equity ratio is one way of institutionalizing that attitude with some discipline. When one's survival is in question, better husbanding of resources, sharper focus, and quicker response to changing market conditions could be expected. However, as always, leveraging beyond a prudent level of debt, even under the more competitive environment, would spell disaster. The question is whether the leveraged buyouts, debt-financed takeovers, and corporate restructurings of the 1980s have pushed U.S. companies into acquiring more debt than is prudent. The leveraging of the corporate balance sheet as a response to competitive pressures portends one certain outcome: the rate of corporate bankruptcy or near bankruptcy will increase in the future. Ability to restructure companies close to bankruptcy ("workout investing") or reorganize companies that have declared bankruptcy would, therefore, be a sought-after skill in the future.

The $25.07 billion purchase of RJR Nabisco, the 19th-largest U.S. industrial company, on December 1, 1988, by Kohlberg Kravis Roberts & Company, an investment partnership, was the largest takeover in U.S. corporate history. The purchase price amounts to $100 for every man, woman, and child in the United States. KKR won out over the management-led leveraged buyout offer of $25.42 billion. If the management had been successful this would have been the largest buyout ever in U.S. corporate history. The failed management offer raises the credible level of leveraged buyouts to stratospheric levels. In the post RJR Nabisco world, barring a handful of U.S. corporations, no corporate entity merely due to its size can be thought of as immune to a management leveraged buyout offer.

The gargantuan RJR Nabisco deal followed closely on the heels of the $5.1 billion bid for Pillsbury by Britain's Grand Metropolitan PLC and the $11 billion takeover of Kraft by Phillip Morris. How do these huge purchases get financed?

Out of the $25 billion offered by KKR for RJR Nabisco, only $1.5 billion would come from a KKR-led equity fund with a public issue of $4.1 billion of preferred stock. The balance of $19.4 billion (78%) will be in the form of commercial bank loans, convertible debenture issues, and bridge loans by the Wall Street firms of Drexel Burnham and Merrill Lynch. The bridge loan of $5 billion will subsequently be repaid with issues of high-yield "junk" bonds. All these deals require significant infusions of debt capital; a debt/equity ratio of approximately 4:1. By the end of 1988, nonfinancial companies will have nearly doubled their debt, to $1.8 trillion, and retired more than $400 billion in equity—all in only six years. The corporate interest bill in 1988 equaled nearly 24% of corporate cash flow—a debt-service burden seen only during cash-strapped recessions—and the economy had not even entered the recessionary phase. For the nonfinancial corporations the interest payments form a much higher 35% of cash flow. This is higher than the 32% interest expense ratio seen in the most recent recession of 1981–82. What does all this forebode for the financial health of corporate America?

During the biggest bull market in history (1982–87), corporate America retired $285 billion more equity in takeovers, buyouts, and share repurchases than it created by floating stock. Financial leverage (ratio of debt to equity) of the nonfinancial corporate sector has risen dramatically from the 48% of 1952 to almost 93% of 1987. The net interest payments of nonfinancial corporations now account for more than 50% of their aggregate pretax earnings; in the 1950s and 1960s the ratio was just 15%, and even in the 1970s it rose to only 30%.

Some analysts have maintained that the current law encourages companies to take on debt because it allows them to deduct their interest payments but not the dividends they pay on stock. At the time of going to press, Treasury Secretary Nicholas Brady had launched a study of measures to encourage U.S. businesses to focus more on long-term competitiveness and less on short-term profits. One of the issues the Treasury is looking at is to determine whether tax laws might be changed to discourage excessive indebtedness. At least five Senate and House panels are planning to hold hearings in 1989 on LBOs and other debt-creating takeovers. However, the Senate committees and the tax-writing panels are none too eager to propose legislation to withdraw tax deductibility advantage of interest payments on debt. Part of the reluctance is due to the belief that the legislation proposed on October 14, 1987, to eliminate certain takeover tax breaks contributed to the stock market crash of October 19, 1987. Moreover, the legislators believe that the withdrawal of deductibility of interest on debt incurred in a buyout could only give foreigners a hefty advantage in takeovers because they often would still enjoy interest write-offs on their home country taxes. Thus when all is said and done, many think that leveraged megadeals are here to stay. The RJR Nabisco megadeal may just have ushered in a new era of supersized leveraged takeovers with increasing tolerance of the leveraged corporate America of the 1990s.

The unspoken question on everyone's mind is: Do the currently high levels of leverage of corporate America portend a tidal wave of bankruptcies at the next recession, possibly in 1990? The increasing popularity of workout investing is indicative of the natural phase that follows the extraleveraging of the corporate balance sheet. Are there lessons to be learned for the investor and the firm from the experiences of the bankruptcies of the 1980's? The impending bankruptcies could pose a problem to the private sector of the same magnitude, if not larger, as the $150 billion savings and loan industry bailout currently facing the public sector (Federal Home Loan Bank Board, Federal Savings and Loan Insurance Corporation, and the Federal Deposit Insurance Corporation).

BANKRUPTCIES: CORPORATE AND PERSONAL

The notion of bankruptcy is rooted in Roman law. The word comes from the Latin for "broken bench"; Roman creditors would physically break a debtor's bench as a punishment and as a warning to other tradesmen.[1] Today's debtors do not suffer the inconvenience or the indignity of their furniture broken.

The United States has come a long way from the Roman law of bankruptcy. The largest corporate bankruptcy in U.S. history was filed on April 12, 1987 by the oil giant, Texaco. The oil company, with $35 billion in assets in 1987, sought bankruptcy protection to forestall enforcement of a $10.3 billion judgment against it awarded to Pennzoil by a Texas jury in December 1985. Prior to the jury verdict Texaco was a healthy company and an unlikely candidate for bankruptcy filing. Some of the biggest corporate bankruptcies are given in Table 1.1. Except for Penn Central all of them occurred in the 1980s. Some 17,142 companies filed for bankruptcy in 1987—nearly triple the 6,298 companies that filed in 1980, says the Administrative Office of the U.S. Courts. Many firms today see Chapter 11 of the federal Bankruptcy Code as the best way to address their business problems when creditors come knocking; under Chapter 11, they get protection from creditors while working out a plan of reorganization.

The bankruptcy code has become an increasingly popular management tool for companies seeking not only protection from creditors but also as a bargaining ploy in their confrontations with the labor unions. Continental Airlines, LTV, and, more recently, Eastern Airlines are instances of this use of the bankruptcy act. Continental Airlines was supposed to have used the bankruptcy act to transform itself into a low-cost nonunion airline after repudiating all labor union contracts consequent to the filing. However, recent changes to the Bankruptcy Code adopted by Congress as a result of the Continental bankruptcy filing will bar any

Table 1.1
Biggest Bankruptcies

Company	Assets (in millions)	Date Filed
Texaco	$34,940	4/12/87
Baldwin United	$9,383	9/26/83
Penn Central	$6,851	6/21/70
LTV	$6,307	7/17/86
Eastern Airlines	$3,773	3/9/89
Public Service, NH	$2,639	1/28/88
Manville	$2,298	8/26/82
Revco D.S.	$1,887	7/28/88
Charter Co.	$1,813	4/20/84
McLean Ind.	$1,812	11/24/86
Global Marine	$1,573	1/27/86
Wickes	$1,552	4/24/82
Itel	$1,410	1/9/81

Source: *The Wall Street Journal,* March 10, 1989

unilateral abrogation of union contracts without first proving economic necessity and negotiating with the unions. Two recent examples of product-liability-driven bankruptcy filings are Manville Corporation and A. H. Robins. Texaco sought protection from the bankruptcy court to forestall enforcement of the $10.3 billion judgment against it awarded to Pennzoil by a Texas jury. Even public service utilities have used the bankruptcy code to circumvent rate regulations. Nine months after Public Service Company of New Hampshire became the first major investor-owned utility to seek protection from creditors since the Depression, it disclosed a reorganization plan to escape state regulation that would leave it federally regulated and able to charge ratepayers for its Seabrook nuclear plant whether or not the reactor ever operates.

Symptomatic of the potential for bankruptcy awaiting the leveraged buyouts of the recent past, on July 29, 1988, Revco, one of the nation's largest drugstore chains, filed for protection under Chapter 11 of the federal Bankruptcy Code. This filing made Revco the largest leveraged buyout to fail financially. The filing came just 19 months after the 2,000-store chain was taken private in a $1.3 billion leveraged buyout and about three months after it stopped making interest payments on the high-yield, or "junk bond," debt used to finance the buyout. Another sorry example of the crushing burden imposed by the overload of buyout debt is the Fruehauf Corporation, once the number-one U.S. maker of truck trailers. The company announced on March 28, 1989, a plan to sell itself off in pieces—dismembering one of the 200 largest industrial companies in the U.S.—in order to lighten the crushing weight of $101 million-a-year debt payments.[2] Fruehauf has already informed the Securities and Exchange Commission that it might be technically insolvent by the end of 1989. These events make Fruehauf the biggest buyout flop so far.

Leveraged buyouts that appear shaky are on the increase. As of December 1988, bond analysts and Wall Street deal-makers see a growing number of wobbly leveraged buyouts. Among those they list are Leaseway Transportation Corporation, Morse Shoe, Papercraft Corporation, Gillett Holdings, Synthetic Industries, Trans World Airlines, Metropolitan Broadcasting, Allied Stores Corporation, and Southland Corporation. Indications that the market for junk bonds may be softening became clear when in October 1988, for the first time, First Boston Corporation had to pull back a $1.15 billion junk bond offering by Campeau Corporation-owned Federated Department Stores after too many investors shunned the high-risk, high-yield issue. A revised $750 million offering at higher yields was not fully subscribed.

Personal bankruptcy (as opposed to commercial bankruptcy) also is becoming quite chic in the United States. Nelson Bunker Hunt, who as recently as the early 1980s was one of the world's richest people, and William Herbert Hunt, one of his brothers, filed in October 1988 for personal bankruptcy under Chapter 11—almost certainly the largest personal bankruptcy filing in U.S. history. They were part of a large crowd of almost 500,000 Americans who filed for personal bankruptcy, up from fewer than 200,000 a year in the late 1970s and from an average of 50,000 in the 1950s. A recent report by the Federal Reserve Board suggested that over half the increase in bankruptcies in the early 1980s was the result of a change in the law in 1978.[3] This gave debtors more protection against claims on their assets. One other major reason cited by the report is the increasing pool of potential debtors: the ratio of consumer debt to income has risen from 7% in 1950 to 19% in 1987. (These figures exclude mortgage debt, which is seldom a cause of bankruptcy since a lender's claim on a mortgaged property is unaffected by a filing for bankruptcy.) Are we becoming a nation of debtors with an incentive to be financially imprudent? Are the costs, restraints, and penalties of playing fast and loose with personal and business fortunes being steadily eroded and eliminated?

THE MARKET FOR HIGH-RISK INVESTMENTS

Despite the litany of complaints against the "overleveraging" of corporate America, the pace of debt-financed mergers and acquisitions and LBOs did not slow down in 1988. Just the opposite. We can investigate investor interest in risky, high-yield securities by considering the three distinct securities markets separately. The first market is the takeovers and capital-restructuring-related high-yield securities markets of bonds and equity. The next is the world of pre-bankruptcy workouts. And finally is the investible market of securities of bankrupt firms.

Mergers and Acquisitions, LBOs, Restructurings, and the High-Yield Market

How has the investor perceived the increasing indebtedness of corporate America? Based on available objective evidence on the demand for high-yield securities, the increased indebtedness of corporate America does not seem to have cooled the fervent reception accorded these securities by the investor. Despite the gigantic size of debt financing required in the takeover of RJR Nabisco, Drexel Burnham has so far successfully financed the bridge loan portion of the deal with high-yield notes. It even increased the amount of $6.5 billion from the targeted $3.0 billion. Drexel found 370 buyers for the RJR high-yield notes compared to 100 buyers for the previous record junk bond offering of $2.5 billion that Drexel masterminded in 1986 to help take Beatrice private. All the while Drexel was under the cloud of criminal indictment for securities fraud and racketeering charges brought by the Securities and Exchange Commission!

LBO and acquisition-related high-yield corporate debt issues as a percentage of the high-yield debt market has risen from 5.3% in 1981 to 57.1% in 1988. The number of investment-grade bonds that have become "fallen angels" (downgraded to high-yield) in the three years 1985–87 is more than $30 billion. This can happen because of takeovers, LBOs, or defensive recapitalizations, where debt is issued to buy back equity. The junk bond market is now about $195 billion. Who are the typical buyers of junk bonds? Insurance companies account for some 30%, mutual funds for another 30%, pension funds 15%, thrifts 8%, and Japanese and other investors the remaining 17%. LBO exposure of the top 21 U.S. commercial banks is estimated at about $40 billion. RJR Nabisco financing alone would entail bank lending of $12 billion; this is equivalent to nearly 70%

of the increase in commercial and industrial loans in 1988 in the United States.

Yet another measure of the interest and demand that investors have for equities of leveraged companies is measured by the performance of an index of equity "stubs." The "stub" is the small amount of stock outstanding in companies that have switched mainly to debt financing. A stub index constructed from the equities of FMC, Fruehauf, USG, Holiday, Multimedia, Owens-Corning, HBJ, and Viacom would have outperformed Standard & Poor's 500 index since 1986.[4]

Pre-Bankruptcy Workout Investors

There are several variations in the common theme of investing in bankrupt or near-bankrupt firms. One form of investment calls for investing in firms that are on the threshold of disaster (uncharitably labeled "vulture capitalism"). Such investments are neither for the faint-hearted nor for the very short-term oriented investor. Such investors (workout investors) invest in defaulted bonds ("busted bonds") bought at bargain-basement prices and hope to reap rich rewards when the firm turns around. Many a time the firm enters bankruptcy and these bond investors then ensure favorable outcome by getting themselves on workout committees and shape the eventual reorganization. Restructuring negotiations always tend to be adversarial. According to one workout banker, "a workout is not as easy as everyone thinks. They are highly stressful. It's not a Wall Street white-shoe business."

Workout investment requires taking a position in "fallen angels" (originally issued as investment-grade bonds that have since become junk or defaulted) and either through exchange offers (i.e., swapping the junk bonds for a higher valued new package of debt and equity) or through reemergence from Chapter 11 bankruptcy reap the rich rewards of the investment. For example, in 1987 Dart Drug Stores, burdened by too much debt from its leveraged buyout the previous year, had offered to exchange its deeply discounted junk bond then valued at $350 (face value of $1,000) for a package of debt, equity, and preferred stock worth over $700. The new bond alone was worth $500. Such exchange offers do not always succeed in convincing enough (80% at least) lenders to prevent the firm from filing Chapter 11 bankruptcy. This is what happened with Revco in 1988 when its public bondholders refused to swap its $700 million junk bonds for Revco's stocks. However, the increasing availability of fallen angels ($21.4 billion of corporate debt in 1987, up from $11 billion in 1984) makes workout investment a viable investment strategy for large funds.

The guiding motive in workout investing is still to avoid the cumbersome and expensive process of bankruptcy filing and subsequent reorganization. Drexel Burnham Lambert, perhaps the most experienced investment bank in the workout arena, has restructured hundreds of companies by exchanging the outstanding junk bonds for zero-coupon, pay-in-kind debt or equity. Most of the Wall Street firms are now participants in this market. Many even risk their capital by investing in troubled companies. Merrill Lynch invested its own $22 million in restructuring Massey-Ferguson, renamed Verity Corporation. For the Wall Street firms, workout investments along with their mergers and acquisitions activities have become part of their merchant banking operations.

The high level of participation and interest has made this market for high-yield security very liquid. While the once high expected returns from investing in securities of distressed firms may have come down as a consequence of the new cash flow into the workout business, the market for selling bad debts and other defaulted business loans has become more liquid. (For instance, a subordinated debenture of the recently bankrupted Revco was trading at 26 cents on the dollar, while based on the company's fundamentals, according to some bankruptcy veterans, it should be trading at no more than 5 to 10 cents on the dollar.) This should help banks in unloading their ample portfolios of nonperforming loans. In short, investor appetite for high-yield security remains high.

It is now generally believed that exchange offers (pre-bankruptcy workouts) will become increasingly rare, and Chapter 11 more frequent. Some of the reasons offered are: first, the public debt is trading too high, owing to increased interest in workout investment from the newer entrants of Wall Street firms; second, pre-bankruptcy exchange offers are generally successful only when there is a single tranche of public debt: out-of-court settlements are feasible. With the more recent generation of LBOs that have more layers of debt and hence too many competing constituencies, exchange offers are more difficult to conclude. This is cited as the primary reason for the unsuccessful attempt at exchange offers for Revco, Public Service Company of New Hampshire, and LTV.

For the workout investor, the future appears to hold out more opportunities for investing in bankrupt companies than in participating in the pre-bankruptcy exchange offers. This requires careful analysis and assessment of the survival probabilities of firms filing Chapter 11. How has the investment market been for securities of bankrupt firms?

Popularity of Investing in Bankrupt Firms

Commitments to distressed company investments could reach $1.5 billion if the new limited partnership funds in the market meet their targets. About $1 billion of this is expected to be invested during the next two years. The investors include corporate pension funds such as Warner-Lambert and Dayton Hudson; endowments and foundations such as The

Rockefeller Foundation; insurance companies like Monumental; and several public pension funds. Cash-rich utilities are said to be the new investors in this area. Oppenheimer is also said to be marketing an investment fund targeted at foreign institutions.[5]

All these investors are expecting average returns of 40% to 50%. Some bankruptcy fund managers feel that investments in bankrupt firms are likely to be a source of diverse, quality investment opportunities. This is based on the assumption that LBOs are the prime candidates for future bankruptcies in an economic downturn and that their turnaround would not require any operational improvements but merely a shrinkage in their debt levels. Chapter 11 is designed for just such a situation. Investment in bankruptcy securities is claimed to provide diversification benefits due to the low correlation of the performance of bankrupt companies with the broad market movements. Yet another reason cited for the popularity of investment in bankrupt companies is the inclusion in that category of Texaco, Manville, A. H. Robins, and others, that adopted bankruptcy for reasons other than financial health.

The stellar performance of some past bankruptcies whose securities, like the Phoenix, have risen from the ashes and soared skyward are also part of the reason for the widening reception of bankruptcy stocks in the investor community. Some ten years ago the big retailer Toys "R" Us emerged from the Interstate Department Stores bankruptcy with its stock trading at 12.5 cents a share. As of 1989, its stock was trading at $38. A similar, successful, more recent story in the fixed income market is that of Storage Technology's 11.625% bonds sold for $500 per $1,000 of face value after the high-tech company filed for bankruptcy in 1984. As it came out of bankruptcy in 1987, the bonds were selling at $1,300.

Betting on bankruptcies requires patient analysis. Legal briefs, fine print on bond indentures, and footnotes in accounting statements all have to be closely researched to dig out the security that is most likely to retain its face value through the bankruptcy process. The following interesting stories highlight the diligence required in picking the right bankruptcy security.

The trick is not just to identify the company; the real talent lies in seeking out the security likely to make the most money. The chief operating officer of R.D. Smith, a New York brokerage firm specializing in the investment of bankrupt securities, figures that at Texaco it's the 10% debentures; at Public Service of New Hampshire it's 17.5% debentures. . . . Take the case of Dome Petroleum, the Canadian company sent reeling by its bet that oil was heading for $100 a barrel. An analyst with R.D. Smith saw that the fine print in one of Dome's many debt offerings—unsecured 14.75% debentures due in 2006 for the driller's Hudson Bay unit—stated that if any other Hudson Bay debt was secured, these bonds would become secured as well. Continuing to search, the analyst found that a group of banks led by Citicorp had made the company a secured loan.

Further research showed that the Hudson Bay debentures were backed by valuable assets and consequently were worth more than par. At the time the analyst made the discovery, the bonds sold for 75 cents on the dollar. Smith & Co. bid on the bonds but never corralled the thinly traded issue. Now the secret is out, and the bonds are selling at par, a 53% return (profit plus accrued interest over a year) for nimble investors.[6]

In 1970 the investment community was shocked when one morning Penn Central Railroad filed for bankruptcy. Wall Street began a mass selling of the company's common stock and its bonds. However, as institutional and income-oriented investors dumped the company's securities, a group of investors, known usually as speculators, gambled that the U.S. Congress would rescue the company. These gamblers began buying the securities, which were trading at very low prices. Not only did these investors believe that the government would not allow a regulated firm to collapse, but they also performed a careful analysis of the company's financial fundamentals. There was the possibility that the securities were trading at prices lower than they were worth. In other words, these speculators felt the securities were undervalued. If a security is selling at a bargain price then there is a high probability that an investor purchasing such a security can later sell it for a large dollar gain.

To arrive at the notion that the firm's securities were undervalued, potential Penn Central investors could have considered some of the following questions when reviewing the firm's financial statements:

- How much debt did Penn Central have?
- How much of the debt was secured with assets?
- Can the assets that were in the form of railroad cars, equipment, land, and track right-of-ways be sold for cash?
- If sold, would these assets bring in more cash than the amount owed debtholders?

In bankruptcy many firms discover that their assets often have a much higher market value than their book value. The book value of an asset is calculated by taking the original cost of an asset and subtracting each year's depreciation. For example, one of Penn Central's railroad locomotives may be valued on the books at $500,000, but because of price inflation and market conditions in the locomotive business it could be sold for $600,000. Thus, the company's value would be higher in actual dollars than the books indicated. This extra value over book was especially apparent to investors when they analyzed the value of the track rights-of-way. Other railroad companies placed a high value on the land that already has railroad tracks on it. To buy land and place tracks on it at current land and labor prices is an extremely expensive undertaking.

Penn Central's track beds were a very valuable asset and were even more so if the railroad was allowed to keep running as a going concern. Speculators who gambled by buying Penn Central bonds after the company filed for bankruptcy were rewarded for their efforts. A secured Penn Central debenture sold for $200 immediately after the firm filed for bankruptcy and could be sold for $1,200 after the announcement of the Penn Central reorganization plan. The bonds provided an annual average return of 100 percent per year for about five years.

The 1980s have sparked much more interest in the bonds and stocks of bankrupt firms as investment opportunities than during the 1970s. Individuals and the managers of speculative mutual funds have been buying these securities for a number of reasons:

- The recession and high interest rates of the early 1980s provided investors with a large group of bankrupt firms to choose from.
- More managements filed for court protection of their companies' assets from creditor claims during the early 1980s than filed during the worst Depression years of the 1930s.
- Although more companies have failed recently than in the past, their financial positions at the time of filing have been much stronger.
- This change may be the result of firms filing under the new bankruptcy law, which became effective in 1978.
- The new law allows firms to file for Chapter 11 of the National Bankruptcy Law as soon as they have insufficient cash flow to pay their bills. Before 1978 firms filed under the old Chapter X law and were required, as a prerequisite to filing, to be insolvent to the point that their liabilities were in excess of their assets. This provision required that managers ran or were allowed to run firms and bleed them of their cash and productive salable assets. The firms that finally filed for Chapter X were often nothing more than empty shells of a business. Creditors would receive ten cents for every dollar of a claim and stockholders would receive nothing. Under the new law, companies can file easily and quickly and can negotiate to have their capital structures reorganized in as little time as one year.
- Finally, filing firms are healthier and investors have a chance of receiving something in the event a firm emerges from Chapter 11 and is reorganized.

Studies have shown that high returns are available from purchasing the bonds and even the stocks of Chapter 11 firms. However, this type of investing is not for the weak hearted because it is risky. Some firms, after entering bankruptcy under Chapter 11, can be forced by the courts and their creditors to liquidate their assets to cash under the Chapter 7 liquidation law. If that occurs, most investors lose their entire investment if they hold the firm's common stocks. They may recoup only 60% or less of the value of their bond investment. So while investing in Chapter 11 securities has become more popular in recent years it is not without its risks.

HOW TO CHOOSE THE BEST INVESTMENT IN BANKRUPT FIRMS

The objective of this book is to help investors interested in buying the securities of bankrupt firms invest in an informed manner. Anyone can read about a company filing for Chapter 11 in *The Wall Street Journal* and tell a broker to buy 100 shares of the stock. The shrewd investor searches for the right bankrupt opportunity by assessing the probability that the stock or bond will yield a substantial return for the investment. Brokers do not usually follow or have much information on the securities of bankrupt firms. It is therefore up to investors to do their own financial analysis of a bankrupt firm's financial statements.

A beginning step in this process would be to obtain the current list of Chapter 11 securities from the Corporate Research Department at the Securities and Exchange Commission in Washington D.C. This information is part of the public record and is available to anyone who writes to the Commission. *The Wall Street Journal* is another source of this information. Common stocks and bonds of bankrupt firms that are still traded on the New York and American Stock Exchanges are indicated in the *Journal* with a 'vj' in front of their names. Securities of firms in bankrupt proceedings that are traded in the National Market System (NASDAQ) are denoted with a fifth letter identifier 'Q.' Current articles on companies considering filing for Chapter 11 relief may allow an investor a chance to begin following the bankruptcy process, and may provide the investor with some information on a firm's financial position.

Actual financial information on a company can be found in the company's annual report or in the appropriate volume of *Moody's Industrial Manuals*. Table 1.2 shows some financial characteristics a potential investor may wish to collect when developing a profile of a Chapter 11 firm. After gathering all available financial information on a specific bankrupt firm, an investor needs to analyze the risk of such an investment. The rest of this book is intended to help investors perform this analysis.

Table 1.3 lists a few bonds of bankrupt firms that were traded as of 1988. Not all bonds were discounted to the same extent; the prices varied from 10 to 54 cents per dollar face value of the bond. The investor would need to perform more financial analysis of the firms; Global Marine, with the highest coupon rate of 16.125 and longest maturity, is also the one with the lowest price of the bond. Thus, coupon and maturity alone are not sufficient to price these bonds. The investor needs to know more about the probability of reorganization of the firm.

Table 1.2
Financial Characteristics of Bankrupt Firms at Filing

Name	Exchange	Size (Total Assets)	Industry	Debt to Equity	Age	Filing	I or B *	Comments
American International	NYSE	$686.1 mm	Manufacture	1.06	58 yrs	4/82	I	Traded on Pacific as of 5/31/82
Arctic Enterprises	NYSE	$110.1 mm	Manufacture	3.79	19 yrs	2/81	I	Traded on Pacific as of 2/23/81
Bobbie Brooks	NYSE	$87.0 mm	Manuf (Retail)	1.93	36 yrs	1/82	I	Traded OTC as of 12/31/81
Empire Oil & Gas	OTC	$31.3 mm	Contract Drilling	1.41	6 yrs	9/82	I	
Fashion Two–Twenty	OTC	$4.7 mm	Manuf (Retail)	0.30	20 yrs	12/81	I	Became privately–held 9/82
HRT	NYSE	$245.7 mm	Retailing	2.77	1 yr**	11/82	I	
Inforex	OTC	$50.6 mm	Manufacture (Computer)	(8.38)	11 yrs	10/79	B	Acquired by Datapoint 9/80
Keydata	OTC	$7.3 mm	Data Processing	(4.71)	20 yrs	10/80	B	
Lawhorn	OTC	$8.3 mm	Retail	2.9	10 yrs	2/81	I	
Lionel	NYSE	$171.3 mm	Manufacture	2.64	64 yrs	2/82	I	
Manville	NYSE	$2297.9 mm	Manufacture	0.91	56 yrs	8/82	I	
National Shoes	OTC	$52.1 mm	Retail	1.46	46 yrs	12/80	I	
Penn Dixie	NYSE	$176.7 mm	Manufacture	2.17	54 yrs	4/80	I	Traded on OTC as of 5/7/80—suspended trading 4/21 – 5/6/80
Revere Ware Copper	NYSE	$473.8 mm	Manufacture	1.51	54 yrs	10/82	I	
SBE	OTC	$1.5 mm	Manufacture	(6.61)	18 yrs	11/79	B	

14

Sambos	NYSE	$276.3 mm	Restaurant	367.36	20 yrs	12/81	B	Traded on Pacific as of 12/10/81
Sam Solomon	OTC	$45.3 mm	Retail	2.51	8 yrs	10/80	I	Acquired by Service Merch. 8/11/82
Saxon	NYSE	$486.6 mm	Manufacture	2.90	58 yrs	4/82	I	Traded on Pacific as of 4/28/82
Seatrain	NYSE	$913.4 mm	Transportation	(84.15)	15 yrs	2/81	B	Traded on Pacific as of 2/26/81
South Atlantic	NYSE	$28.6 mm	Inv. management	2.5	3 yrs**	10/82	I	Traded on OTC as of 11/26/82—suspended trading 8/25/82 – 11/25/82
UNR	NYSE	$232.6 mm	Manufacture	2.46	2 yrs	7/82	I	Traded on OTC as of 9/8/82—suspended trading 8/12/82 – 9/7/82
Unishelter	OTC	$13.8 mm	Land Develop.	101.51	20 yrs	8/81	I	Liquidated 11/82
Van Wyck	OTC	$9.2 mm	Marketing	(5.27)	15 yrs	2/80	B	New name (Robeson) on OTC beginning 7/82
Wickes	NYSE	$1705.3 mm	Holding Company	4.25	2 yrs	4/82	I	Trading on Pacific as of 5/7/82

* : Insolvent (I) or Bankrupt (B) at the time of filing.
** : Since the last reorganization.

Table 1.3
A Sample of Bankruptcy Bonds

Issuer*	Coupon rate	Year of maturity	Price per $100 of face value
Allegheny International	10.40%	2002	52
Basix	11.625	2003	33½
Coleco	14.375	2002	18
De Laurentis Entertainment	12.50	2001	10
Global Marine	16.125	2003	10
LTV	13.875	2002	$46\frac{5}{8}$
Public Service of New Hampshire	15.00	2003	43
Revco	13.125	1994	54

* All have filed for Chapter 11 protection from creditors and are not paying interest on the bonds.

Source: *Business Week*, September 5, 1988

ORGANIZATION OF THE BOOK

Chapter 2 outlines the benefits of investing in bankrupt stocks. Studies are cited whose results show that it is possible to earn large absolute dollar returns from such investing. Practical ways of investing in bankrupt securities are outlined. Itel Corporation's reorganization plan is highlighted as evidence that these large absolute returns may be excessive. These returns may be higher than they should be for the risk of the investment. A section on high-yield (junk) bonds compares and distinguishes the high-risk worlds of the junk bonds (LBOs, highly leveraged takeovers, and small, unknown growth company issues), the securities of bankrupt firms and the new, emerging world of workout investing (issues of companies that are rescued, as it were, from the jaws of bankruptcy).

Chapter 3 describes the economic environment in which a Chapter 11 firm must operate. Reasons that firms fail are discussed and illustrated with examples of situations that result in firms entering financial distress. The impact of financial distress on a company's securities, as well as the effect of reorganization on a firm's value, is also covered. The chapter is important as it explains why investors should expect excess returns from an investment in a bankrupt stock or bond.

Chapter 4 summarizes the provisions of the old and new bankruptcy laws. This chapter provides further evidence that it may be possible for investors to invest and earn excess returns from the securities of bankrupt firms.

Chapter 5 analyzes studies that have been performed on the post-bankruptcy performance of bankrupt firm securities. It shows evidence that if a bankrupt stock is purchased after the firm files for Chapter 11, and is held through the time in which the firm is reorganized, then large absolute dollar returns can be earned. Since liquidation of a firm's assets usually results in a loss to investors, this chapter examines the results of a study that presents a model on how to choose companies that will successfully reorganize. The model is a probabilistic model based on logit analysis.

Chapter 6 presents additional research that has been done on how the stock market reacts to a firm in financial distress. The research provides insights into when the stock price of a bankrupt firm is first affected by financial distress announcements by management. The authors hope that this book will provide investors who have an interest in speculative investment with some practical tips on how and when to choose bankrupt securities for investment purposes and with some theoretical background on the academic research in the field.

Chapter 7 presents four case studies—MCorp, Manville Corporation, Massey-Ferguson of Canada, and Texaco. MCorp, a more recent (1988) case study in the savings and loans (S&L) industry, is presented to indicate the potential for high returns from investment in bankrupt securities. Important legal issues involving the roles of the FDIC and the Federal Reserve in fulfilling their respective mandates and the resultant impact on the risk of investing in bankrupt securities of S&Ls are also highlighted. Manville Corporation illustrates the enormous bankrupting potential of product liability cases. Investors in such securities need to evaluate the latent magnitude of the liability, available insurance coverage, and ability of the firm to survive in markets unrelated to the product under seige. Massey-Ferguson illustrates the technique of computing the probability of bankruptcy from published financial ratios of the firm. This case also describes the failure of management to anticipate the special nature and problems of its customer's market. Texaco is a study in gross underestimation and misjudgment of the legal ramifications of contested mergers and acquisitions.

NOTES

1. *The Economist,* October 29, 1988, p. 73.
2. See *The Wall Street Journal,* March 29, 1989.
3. Federal Reserve Bulletin, "Personal Bankruptcies," Charles A. Luckett, September 1988, pp. 591–603.
4. *Business Week,* November 7, 1988, p. 141.
5. *Pensions and Investment Age,* March 6, 1989, p. 1.
6. *Fortune,* February 15, 1988, p. 101.

Shrewd Investors and Bankrupt Firms

Institutional and retail, conservative and aggressive investors gain from an understanding of the nature of bankrupt firms. A study by Altman (1987) indicated that the risk of junk bonds of high-yield, high-risk securities (as measured by the relative default rates of bonds of different risk classifications) is typically overestimated by the capital markets leading to high returns to junk bond holders. A similar reaction of the capital markets to securities of bankrupt firms could afford prescient investors an opportunity to earn high returns. In this chapter we will investigate whether investment in bankrupt firms does typically yield high returns. We will also consider the related high-yield junk bond market, the different types of high-yield securities including those created by the LBOs, the highly leveraged takeovers, and corporate capital restructurings. This chapter also contains a description of the leveraged buyout process.

INCENTIVE TO FILE BANKRUPTCY

Bankruptcy filings have been up significantly since 1980.[1] It has become an increasingly popular management tool for companies to seek protection from creditors. Some have even sought to use it as a bargaining ploy in their confrontations with the labor unions. Eastern Airlines, Continental Airlines, and LTV are some recent instances of this use of the bankruptcy act. Sometimes a Chapter 11 filing is made primarily to void leases, contracts, or lawsuits that threaten to undermine a company's solvency. (Congress as a result of the Continental Airlines bankruptcy filing adopted stiffer requirements before unilaterally abrogating union contracts; now, the company must first prove economic necessity and a good faith attempt to negotiate with the unions.) Two recent examples are Manville, which filed for protection against asbestos-related lawsuits, and A.H. Robins, whose Dalkon Shield birth-control device is alleged to have caused severe injuries. The largest bankruptcy proceeding in U.S. history was filed by Texaco on April 11, 1987 in order to forestall enforcement of a $10.3 billion judgment against it awarded Pennzoil by a Texas jury in December 1985. Both Texaco and A.H. Robins have now emerged from bankruptcy proceedings as reorganized firms. While Texaco retained its identity, A.H. Robins was acquired by American Home Products. A successful reorganization can provide investors with handsome returns, but investing in bankruptcies is not a step to be taken lightly.

Chapter 3 investigates the reasons for failure of firms and the consequent need to file for bankruptcy. Here, we recognize the fact that the 1978 Bankruptcy Reform Act has made it easier and less traumatic for management to file for Chapter 11. Managements no longer need to prove that their firms are insolvent.[2] Instead, a poor actual or expected cash flow position provides enough justification for the courts to order that distressed firms be protected from their creditors. The new law also allows managers to retain control and maintain their positions in a Chapter 11 firm. Under the old law, Chapter X, trustees replaced upper-echelon executives and operated bankrupt corporations for the benefit of the creditors. The court now views reorganizing firms as "going-concerns" and is interested that all investors in these firms receive something from reorganization. The old "absolute-priority" rule, which established the priority of claimants with debtholders above shareholders, is gone. Today, the court encourages claimants to work together with a reorganizing firm's management. More negotiation takes place between creditors and equityholders, often resulting in equityholders receiving shares in a reorganizing firm when it emerges from Chapter 11.

INCENTIVE TO INVEST IN BANKRUPT FIRMS

It is no secret that as a company enters financial distress the risk for its shareholders increases. The stock market heavily discounts the equity; selling pressure mounts for the troubled stock, and the price falls. The question for someone interested in investing in troubled stocks is when has the stock price bottomed out? Similarly, for the potential bondholders, the incentive to invest in a high-yield debt will be a function of the probability of reorganization of the bankrupt firm and the subsequent chances of its healthy survival.

Investment in Equity of Bankrupt Firms

Academic research has demonstrated that the bottom price does not result until the firm formally files for Chapter 11. There may be market reassessments of the solvency position of failed firms four to six years prior to their filing for bankruptcy (see chapter 6 for a more detailed discussion on the stock market perception of impending bankruptcies), but most research (see Altman 1969b; Westerfield, 1970; Aharony et al., 1980; and Clark and Weinstein 1983) indicates that failure itself was not expected by the stock market players. Instead, the market displays a strong negative reaction when a firm finally declares its intent to file for Chapter 11—more stock is sold off, and the price falls even lower.

Edward Altman, the academic father of bankruptcy research, sums up market reaction when he says,

It was found that the price of bankrupt firm equities falls on average 25% from one month before failure to one month after. This drop in price, sometimes referred to as the bankruptcy information effect, implies that the market was not totally anticipating the bankruptcy, or else the price would have been fully discounted (Altman, 1969, p. 132).

Some large firms are able to reorganize capital structure through out-of-court settlements. Chrysler Corporation and International Harvester are two examples. Others, however, must file for Chapter 11 protection or be forced into liquidation by creditors. The purpose of reorganization in this case is to allow negotiations to occur between debtor firms and their creditors under the supervision of the bankruptcy court.

Clearly, the effect of this process on a firm's future earning power is important to investors and management. At any time during the negotiations, the court can rule that the firm must be liquidated. The length of time a firm remains in reorganization depends on the extent of its problems as well as the willingness of creditors and courts to support it until reorganization. The Chapter 11 firms that emerge from reorganization usually are smaller. They have little debt, and sometimes they have a new name. Others may be acquired by another firm. Obviously, financial distress may not be fatal for a firm.

A successful reorganization that brought wealth for shareholders is Interstate Stores. The company was quoted as low as 12.5 cents in 1975 after it filed under Chapter 11. An investor who bought the stock then would now own shares of Toys "R" Us, the reorganized company, which traded as high as $41.375 per share in 1978. Investors who bought $37,000 worth of W.T. Grant bonds in June 1976 were rewarded with $300,000 in cash six years later when the company completed its liquidation and settled its lawsuits. On the downside, equityholders received nothing from the liquidation. On April 4, 1982, Wickes stock was at $2.25 per share. By November 4, 1982, the stock had risen in value to $6 per share. An investor holding the stock for seven months would have reaped almost a 300 percent return. Since that time, investors have done even better. Share price of A.H. Robins rose steadily from about $8.50 in August 1985, when the company filed for protection to freeze thousands of suits brought by women who claimed injury from the company's Dalkon Shield intrauterine contraceptive, to $24.875 by January 1988.

Investors are interested in bankrupt stocks because there is always some value left in the company. As recently as 1981, short-term investment in companies in Chapter 11 totaled about $100 million a year. By 1988 it had risen to about $1.2 billion.[3] Many institutional investors no longer drop companies automatically when they enter Chapter 11. Private investor groups, brokerage houses, and specialized mutual funds are pouring money into Chapter 11 companies. Their hope is that restructuring will increase share prices. For instance, by 1988 Carl Icahn, an investor, had racked up paper profits of at least $143 million on his Texaco shares. Wall Street analysts estimated that speculators in A.H. Robins stock, such as Steinhardt Partners of New York, saw their holdings increase in value by tens of millions of dollars.

Yet, there is plenty of risk—and often a long wait—before an investor can cash in on a bankrupt buy. The problem is to estimate what value is left, to learn how many creditors there are and who has prior claim, and to figure out how much, if anything, will be left for the stockholders. However, owing to the increased investment and interest of investors in bankrupt firms, shareholder "equity committees" have begun to exert great influence on the outcome of the reorganization process. In Texaco's bankruptcy case, a committee representing shareholders accomplished in a few weeks what the combatants couldn't in four years of legal conflict: the group galvanized a $3 billion compromise settlement of the company's $10.3 billion fight with Pennzoil.[4]

Information about bankrupt issues is often sketchy, rumors abound, and in the case of bonds the buy and sell spreads are extreme, often five to ten points. One big advantage of investing in bankrupt stocks is their very limited downside risk—the issues are so cheap. Dealing in options is a good comparison.[5] There is only a limited amount of money to be lost. After filing for bankruptcy, Braniff, for example, traded at 50 cents, AM International at $1.20, and Itel at 75 cents.

Investment in Debt of Bankrupt Firms

According to R.D. Smith & Co., a brokerage firm that specializes in bankrupt securities, the current buyable universe of bankrupt firms is about 40.[6] There are another 30 or so in default on principal or interest and maybe another 50 to 60 whose bonds are yielding 15% to 16%. Returns from bankrupt bonds have typically been high. For instance, the bonds of firms that declared bankruptcy in the 1970s that Altman (1983a) considered ranged in average annual returns from −15% to 45%. More recently, for example, the Towle Manufacturing Company of Boston's 9.5s of 2000 rose from a bankruptcy filing price of about $470 in March 1988 to about $660 by the end of 1988, resulting in a handsome annualized return of 60%. Similarly, Smith International of Newport, California, saw its 9.85s of 2004 rise from the March bankruptcy price of $400 to around $550 by the end of 1988, resulting in an annualized return of about 56%. With business failures on the rise to more than 60,000 in 1988, and an expected Chapter 11 filing of 20,000, the available pool of bankrupt securities to invest in will widen.

Securities of firms that at one time were financially healthy but are since distressed are classified as "fallen angels" in the high-yield debt market. In 1986–87, this sector comprised about 30% of the high-yield market. Even after accounting for defaults, the total rate of return on a diversified portfolio of high-yield issues was a respectable 16.1% in 1986 (see Altman, 1987). More recently, the so-called high-yield, high-risk junk bonds yielded 8.2% during the first half of 1988.[7] This was the highest return among U.S. fixed income securities in the first half of 1988, trailing only Australian and Canadian government bonds in the world's major bond markets. The nine-year 1980–88 (through October) compounded return was 208% for junk bonds, 156% for high-grade corporate bonds, and 182% for long-term Treasury bonds. According to one estimate, Altman (1987), the high yield debt market grew to about $125 billion by April 1987. To the extent that the high-yield market is viewed as comprising securities of firms that are either currently distressed or have a very high potential for financial failure, analysis of this market is the appropriate framework to study the securities of bankrupt firms. Though the securities of bankrupt firms comprise only a fraction of the high-yield market, very high returns of the last few years are indicative of the rich rewards that await the judicious investor in bankrupt firms.

A number of investors have attempted to earn high returns by purchasing the common stocks of firms in reorganization or in financial difficulty. Have the returns been worth the risk? How does the average bankrupt stock compare with the average bankrupt bond? Altman (1983a) found that while the average bankrupt bond earned more than the average corporate bond, the average bankrupt stock underperformed the average corporate stock.

We will investigate the performance of the bankrupt stock and high-yield debt in greater detail later in this chapter. Finally, it is of interest to investors to determine if there are investment management firms or money managers who specialize in the investment of funds in bankrupt firms and high-yield debt (LBOs, debt-financed takeovers, etc.). Do institutions invest in bankrupt firms and high-yield securities? We shall consider these questions next.

Paucity of Market Information

The very lack of information about bankrupt firms makes it possible to reap rich rewards by investing in the stocks of these firms. Investors in bankrupt companies believe that the capital market for Chapter 11 firms is inefficient. One reason that the market may be inefficient is due to a lack of publicly available information about the bankrupt firm. During the reorganization process firms often do not publish annual reports or any financial information. Most firms no longer trade on an organized exchange, or if they do, trading is infrequent. Also large institutional investors sell or abandon their holdings of Chapter 11 stocks, while many financial analysts fail to follow these firms.[8] Therefore, the potential for abnormal returns—returns that are in excess of those needed to compensate investors for their risk—may exist for investors purchasing Chapter 11 stocks after filing because of market inefficiencies.

The flip side of the scarcity of market information about bankrupt firms is that the investor expectations may also be incorrect. Many investors view firms that file for Chapter 11 as becoming riskier. This view is supported by the fact that these firms are usually in financial distress because of management incompetence and/or are carrying too much debt.[9] A new type of risk called reorganization risk could result in an increase in firm risk. This risk deals with the effect of judicial factors that are beyond the control of management, debt negotiation difficulties, and, finally, the question of how the courts would resolve the division of the shrunken pie among the creditors, shareholders, and other claimants. The uncertainty surrounding the distribution of the wealth of a firm will affect the way individual investors perceive the risk of the firm. However, not all investors in reorganizing companies believe that a firm's risk will increase after filing. The reorganization process could reduce the firm-specific risk of the filing firms. Firm-specific risk is defined as the risk arising from factors that are characteristic to a particular company or industry. Court protection from creditor debts could reduce firm-specific risk as it helps strengthen a firm's financial position. Also a decline in specific risk can be expected if higher earnings potential exists after filing because of a lighter debt load, or if management changes the thrust of its investment policies to include less-risky projects.

How to Invest in Bankrupt Firms

For individual investors, Standard & Poor's *Outlook,* in addition to identifying companies in various industries that are in bankruptcy proceedings, has the following good advice:

- Place only a small percentage of your investment funds in shares of bankrupt firms. You should have both the financial and emotional ability to withstand full loss of the money.
- Buy an equal dollar amount of several bankrupt equities in order to diversify risk.
- Confine bankruptcy speculation to those shares listed on the stock exchanges. (This could cut down the investible universe of securities.)
- Buy the shares shortly after the company files for bankruptcy. While at this point of greatest uncertainty the risk is probably the highest, the stock at that time may be the cheapest.
- Invest in firms that appear to have a viable core business.
- Be patient.

In chapter 5 we describe a method to identify the firms that have the best chance for reorganization from among the firms that have filed for bankruptcy. This should help in assessing the risk associated in buying securities of firms that have just recently filed for bankruptcy. Use of Altman's Zeta credit scoring (Z score) model (which is described in chapter 6 in the section on "Financial Analysis and the Bankrupt Firm") has also been shown to add value to expected returns by identifying potential debt defaulters ahead of time.

Institutional investment in bankrupt firms is limited. Fiduciary responsibility and the notion of the "prudent investor" rule effectively limit the investment options available to an institutional fund. More recently, with the recognition that investments in high-yield securities (junk bonds) have been richly rewarding, institutions have been much less reluctant to buy securities of companies in financial difficulty. The $1.8 billion Rockefeller Foundation doubled to $20 million an allocation made earlier to Oppenheimer Capital Corporation of New York for a fund that buys securities of firms in financial difficulty, including some bankruptcies.[10] For individuals who lack the time or means to develop a portfolio of bankrupt firms, there are mutual funds whose investment objectives are to invest in such firms—to name a couple: Max Heine's Mutual Shares Corporation and Merrill Lynch's Phoenix Fund. Among the handful of advisory services that specialize in the securities of financially risky companies are M.J. Whitman & Co. of New York and R.D. Smith & Co. of New York.

Mutual Shares Corporation, which specializes in companies embroiled in mergers, bankruptcy-law proceedings, and other so-called distressed issues, has been one of the best long-term performers around. Assets of Mutual Shares grew from about $4 million in 1975 to nearly $4 billion by 1989. For a 15-year period ending December 1988, Mutual Shares soared nearly 2000% compared with about 450% for the broad securities market index of Standard & Poor's 500 assuming reinvestment of dividends.

Table 2.1
Firms Investing in Distressed Companies

Company	Funds Committed* Millions
Morgens, Waterfall, Vintiadis	$350
Neuberger and Berman	250
Recovery Equity Partners	150
Oppenheimer	145
The Foothill Group	130
T. Rowe Price	107
Trust Co. of the West	100
Paceholder Associates	100
Amroc Investments	60
Whitman Heffernan Rhein	60
Halcyon Investments	25
Calhoun, Meehan & Co.	15

* Numbers represent amounts raised or targeted;

See Appendix 1 for a description of their investment styles

Source: *Pensions & Investment Age*, March 6, 1989

Over the short term the performance has been just as spectacular. Mutual Shares gained 30.16% in 1988 (through December 22), more than double the 14.18% average gain of its growth-and-income fund peers and the approximately 14.5% gain for the S&P index.[11] Over the period 1983–88, the $192 million Merrill Lynch Phoenix Fund, which invests in the securities of distressed firms, has had an annualized return of 16%, a full percentage point ahead of the stock market average.

Institutional investors are beginning to notice the lucrative returns of the magnitude described above. Commitments to distressed company investments could reach $1.5 billion by early 1989, if the new limited partnership funds meet their targets. A list of the investment partnerships or firms created for the purpose of investing in distressed companies is given in Table 2.1.

As mentioned before, corporate pension funds, endowments and foundations, insurance companies, public pension funds, cash-rich utilities and foreign institutions have now begun to invest in distressed company securities. Some factors cited for the current high level of interest in this type of investment are: the more frequent use of the Bankruptcy Code as a business strategy unrelated to financial health, thus leading to a more benign perception of firms filing for bankruptcy; and the expected cash-flow-related (but operationally sound) failure of the LBOs of yesteryear owing to the anticipated recession providing investors with a high-quality, diversified portfolio of investments. The styles of bankruptcy investing range from the diversified portfolio approaches of firms like Oppenheimer and T. Rowe Price to more concentrated investments of Whitman Heffernan Rhein who take large positions in selected bankruptcy securities, to turnaround or recovery investors like Calhoun, Meehan & Co., which acquires troubled firms. The investment managers also buy everything from public debt and equity securities to private bank debt and from senior secured debt to subordinated debt. Appendix 1 contains a brief description of the investment styles of various funds that invest in distressed firms.

Currently, the market for high-yield corporate debt issues is much more active than the "low quality" equity issues. Consequently, there are high-yield debt indexes computed by major Wall Street firms (Drexel, Shearson, Salomon, First Boston, and Merrill Lynch) to follow the performance of this market, whereas there are no similar "low quality" equity indexes at this time. Lipper Analytical Service of New York has a service (Lipper Fixed-Income Fund Performance Analysis) that ranks the performance of mutual funds dedicated to the high-yield fixed income market. Dun & Bradstreet also publishes lists of firms in bankruptcy proceedings.

Do Equity Investors Benefit from Investing in Bankrupt Firms?

What kind of equity returns can investors in bankrupt firms typically expect? Let us look at the holding period returns that were available to equity investors who purchased the stocks of reorganizing firms after filing occurred and held them until a firm was reorganized, liquidated, or merged with another firm. Let us also compare these holding period returns to the calendar holding period returns of Max Heine's Mutual Shares Corporation.[12] (A similar approach was used by Altman [1969] to study the comparative returns of bankrupt stocks and the New York Stock Exchange Index.) This fund is chosen as a proxy for a risk index because it invests in the securities of financially distressed firms. This fund is also chosen as a comparative index since it appears to be well-managed and has performed well in up and down markets. For the last nine years, it has appeared on the *Forbes* honor roll as one of the best performing mutual funds.

Table 2.2
Annualized Returns of Firms after Chapter 11 Filing, 1979–83

Firm	Stock Return (%)	Mutual Shares[*] (%)	Holding Period (Months)
Advent (R)	-76.6	-13.0	13
Airlift International	-24.0	4.4	30
Allied Technology (R)	-19.3	10.7	18
American International	82.8	10.8	29
Arctic Enterprises (R)	348.0	7.2	10
Autotrain (L)	-41.1	0.4	29
Bobbie Brooks (R)	30.5	12.0	13
Colonial Commercial (R)	72.0	3.4	25
Combustion Equipment (R)	-25.0	4.1	47
Computer Communication (R)	-10.2	0.7	33
Data Dimension (R)	120.0	8.7	22
Empire Oil (L)	-100.0	34.0	12
Fashion Two-Twenty (R)	-44.0	-17.3	9
FSC	19.9	6.5	26
Gamex (R)	111.3	26.7	18
Goldblatt Brothers (R)	48.8	8.3	29
Good L. S. (R)	-37.5	2.6	32
HRT	48.9	15.7	13
Inforex (R)	-5.5	15.3	11
Itel (R)	254.6	8.7	33
Keydata (R)	-12.5	-8.5	24
Lafayette Radio (R)	-8.7	3.3	18
Lawhorn (R)	-30.0	-8.0	12
Lionel	32.0	19.4	21
Lynnwear (R)	-6.5	1.0	24
Manville	30.0	22.5	22
Mays (R)	39.8	16.9	23
McLouth Steel (R)	-38.1	3.7	16
Med Pak (L)	-50.0	3.5	24
National Shoes	69.3	3.3	36
NuCorp	-40.2	25.4	17
Penn Dixie (R)	0.0	6.3	21
Revere Ware	12.0	17.1	14
Richton International (R)	3.0	3.0	20
Rusco (R)	120.0	25.6	15
SBE (R)	20.0	14.0	12

Table 2.2 (continued)

Firm	Stock Return (%)	Mutual Shares* (%)	Holding Period (Months)
Sam Solomon (R)	177.5	2.7	24
Sambos	81.5	5.5	9
Saxon	-12.0	14.9	21
Seatrain	14.6	4.4	33
Shelter Resources	-13.6	20.8	15
Stevcoknit (R)	131.3	5.7	17
South Atlantic	73.6	21.6	15
Tenna (L)	-33.3	-0.3	36
Topps and Trowsers (R)	70.4	14.4	15
Unishelter	-80.8	-7.2	15
UNR	105.9	14.0	17
Upson	2.3	-3.7	42
Van Wyck (R)	57.1	10.3	29
Wickes	29.1	-22.1	19
Average	**28.0**	**8.5**	**21.5**
Average Annualized S&P 500		**15.8**	

Note: (R) indicates that a firm was reorganized, while (L) indicates that the firm's assets were liquidated. Twenty seven firms were reorganized as of December 31, 1983. Some firms had not finished reorganization by December 31, 1983. Their holding period returns were calculated as of December 31, 1983.

*: Returns over same holding period as stock; for comparability, returns have been annualized.

Source: Moeller (1986).

A sample of 50 firms was selected from a list of approximately 200 firms that filed for Chapter 11 between October 1, 1979, and December 31, 1983. This list, which represented the population of Chapter 11 firms existing during the time period, was obtained from the Corporate Reorganization Department of the Securities and Exchange Commission, and is available to the public. The sample firms were specifically chosen from the population of Chapter 11 firms based on whether return data and financial information were available. Returns were determined for the stock of each firm, with a buy date of the first day on which a trade could be made after the Chapter 11 filing was announced; the sell date was the legal completion date of the process. The returns covered different holding periods and lasted for varying amounts of time; for comparability, they were annualized.

The results are presented in Table 2.2. The table lists the individual companies included in the sample and their after-filing annualized returns. The second column represents the comparable return for the Mutual Shares fund over the same holding period; these figures have also been annualized.

The following findings can be summarized from the results reported in Table 2.2:

- Average duration of the bankruptcy process from the filing date (i.e., holding period) is 21.5 months.
- Average annual return for the sample of 50 stocks is 28%. The range of returns, however, varied from a gain of 348% to a loss of 100% in value.
- The average return on the firm achieving successful reorganization is a whopping 49%. Clearly, it pays to determine the probability of reorganization before investing in a bankrupt firm. (More of this in chapter 5.)
- Our portfolio of 50 stocks earned on average 19.5% more than the Mutual Shares for the same holding period. The more extensively diversified Mutual Shares would of course have a lower risk.
- The S&P 500 returns (not shown in table) were also determined for each stock's holding period; the average annualized return for the S&P 500 was 15.8%.

To help distinguish which bankrupt stocks could provide the highest absolute return over the Mutual Shares fund, the sample was divided into two groups using the following characteristics: exchange listing before filing, and size of total assets at filing. Table 2.3 shows that most firms that earned a positive premium over the Mutual Shares fund were traded on the NYSE before filing and were large in size. On the other hand, firms that earned less than the fund were more frequently traded over-the-counter before filing and were small in size.

The results show that if an investor had purchased all 50 of the stocks in the sample at the time the management filed for bankruptcy (Chapter

Table 2.3
Characteristics of Firms Different from Mutual Shares

	Number of firms earning more than Mutual Shares	Number of firms earning less than Mutual Shares
Listing		
New York Stock Exchange	13	4
American Stock Exchange	5	7
Over-the-counter	7	14
Size		
Over $100 million	11	6
$25–$100 million	9	9
Under $25 million	5	10

11 protection)—and held them until the companies were officially reorganized, liquidated, or merged into another firm—she or he could have earned high absolute returns over the return that was available on the Mutual Shares or the S&P 500. Furthermore, firms that may earn returns above Mutual Shares, a risky index, are likely to be those listed on the NYSE and have assets over $100 million. One explanation for the large absolute return of the bankrupt firms is that investors were not able to judge accurately the reorganization risk of these firms, and accordingly the stocks were underpriced.

Do Bond Investors Benefit from Investing in Bankrupt Firms?

The investible market for bonds of bankrupt firms is, in all likelihood, limited to bonds rated BB or lower just before default. Out of 130 defaulting debt issues during 1970–84, Altman and Nammacher (1985) found only four that had a rating of BBB or higher six months prior to default. (Manville Corporation had the only A rating; more recently in 1987 it was Texaco). The average annual default rate for the period 1978–87 in this low-rated category of bonds was 1.86%. In dollar amount the par value of defaulted bonds in 1987 for the low rate category was $7.5 billion. Excluding the Texaco bonds that defaulted in 1987, the increase in market supply of defaulted bonds in that year was $1.8 billion. In 1986 the increase in defaulted bond supply was even larger at $3.2 billion. When bank loans are added to public bonds, according to data gathered by T. Rowe Price, in 1984, 51 large companies defaulted on $11 billion in debt and in 1987, 87 companies defaulted on $21.4 billion in debt obligations.

An indication of the potential for high returns from investment in bonds of bankrupt firms is the ability of these bonds to gain back part of their value lost immediately after the default. Altman (1988) found that bonds that defaulted, on the average, kept almost 40% of their original par value. If one assumes that the bonds of firms in distress are likely to be classified as either B or CCC, then Altman's 1988 study on the mortality of bonds suggests that these very risky, low-rated bonds are likely to earn over a period of five years a return spread of between 15% and 20% over Treasuries over one year. Thus, on the average, a well-diversified portfolio of bonds of distressed firms will seem to possess a potential for high returns. Of course, firm-specific bond risk could still be very high.

Most of the defaulted corporate debt has come from the energy, steel, and entertainment sectors. For the period 1970–86, Altman (1987) showed that almost 59% by dollar amount of public bond default was in three industries: general manufacturing (including steel), oil and gas, and railroads, with the proportion of railroads continuing to fall. Some illustrative bankruptcy bond returns are: (1) Storage Technology's 11.625% bonds sold for $500 per $1,000 of face value after it filed for bankruptcy in 1984; emerging from bankruptcy, some 32 months later, the bonds were worth $1,300. (2) Towle Manufacturing's (Boston, Mass.) 9.5% debentures of 2000 declined from around $700 at the time it filed for Chapter 11 to about $470 and has since then climbed back up to around $660. (3) Smith International (Newport Beach, California), producer of oil-country bits and drills saw its 9.85s of 2004 decline from around $600 at the time of bankruptcy filing to about $400 and then rally back to around $550. (4) Texaco's 113/4s of 1994 if bought when it filed for Chapter 11 in April 1987 would have returned approximately 50% by March 1989. Table 1.3 of Chapter 1 shows a sample of bonds of distressed firms that were available in September 1988 at significant discounts to their par values. At least three mutual funds directed toward the retail market— Keystone Series B4, T. Rowe Price High Yield, and Venture Income Plus—invest in bankrupt bonds.

Itel: An Illustrative Reorganization Plan

For investors interested in purchasing Chapter 11 stocks, understanding the impact of a plan for reorganization on a firm's value is important in order to make wise investment decisions. Itel's reorganization plan is described in the following paragraphs as a guide for investors.

At the time the reorganization plan was announced, Itel's bonds were trading at $250. After the details of the plan were made public the price of the bonds rose immediately to $480. Investors who had purchased the bonds at $250 could have earned a return of almost 100 percent over the period of a few days. The risk of these bonds became similar to that of Treasury bills. Creditors who held approximately $780 million in senior unsecured debt at the time Itel made its filing received $228 million in cash plus interest on $221 million that accrued from the filing date of January 1, 1982, until reorganization became final. In summary, the creditors received $350 for every $1,000 invested. The equity portion of the package included $100 million of a new series of preferred stock. Each bondholder received 1,523 shares of this preferred stock, which bankruptcy experts at the firm of Herzog, Heine, and Geduld valued somewhere between $20 and $25 a share or about $30.50 to $38 for each $1,000 bond investment. Bondholders also got 70 percent of the common stock of the reorganized Itel or about 16 shares for every $1,000 bond. With the stock value at between $5 and $8 a share, that translated into between $80 and $128 per bond.

Thus, the value of the equity portion of the package ranged between $110.50 and $166 for each bond. Therefore the total package that bond-holders received was worth $621.50 to $691.00 per $1,000 investment. The bond selling at $480 was clearly undervalued and at $250 before the announcement of the plan was obviously a good buy for investors.

Can we conclude that the capital markets are inefficient in pricing the securities of the bankrupt firms and thus afford profitable opportunities to investors? Are investors in bankrupt firms being overcompensated for the risk they bear in purchasing those equities? We will investigate that question later.

THE MARKET FOR HIGH-YIELD DEBT OR JUNK BONDS

Similar to the securities of bankrupt firms offering the potential for high returns are the debt issues and equity "stubs" issued by firms that are considered less-than-investment grade. These are the so-called high-risk debt issues (junk bonds) that, because of their low quality, offer potentially high returns. Accounting for about one-fourth of all outstanding corporate bonds, the $180 billion junk bond market now includes more than 1,000 companies. Firms that issue such high-risk securities are typically the small, growth-oriented firms that have not yet been recognized as financially strong by the capital markets. (Since less than 4% of U.S. corporations have investment-grade ratings, the companies that issue junk bonds are not necessarily obscure.) Such high-risk securities (debt) are also issued by public firms that have been taken private by a small group of equity shareholders (usually the senior management of the firm) largely through borrowings. These are the so-called leveraged buyouts. In 1986 LBOs accounted for 25% of all primary market issuance of high-yield debt; in 1988 this proportion was 34%. Corporate takeovers of large firms (whether friendly or hostile) have also resulted in the issuance of high-yield debt when the takeover has chiefly been financed with borrowings. More recently, however, the notoriety of this high-yield market is attributable to the fact that firms ("blue chip," investment-grade firms) that were once considered beyond the realm of such leveraged takeovers (takeovers financed largely with borrowings) owing to their sheer size have found to be not so well-insulated after all. The most recent and the biggest of these takeovers was the $25 billion acquisition of the once-blue-chip RJR Nabisco by the investment firm Kohlberg Kravis Roberts. Almost 78% of the acquisition price will be financed through one form of debt or other.

The low-grade, fixed-income securities have grown dramatically and now with over $180 billion outstanding represent almost one-quarter of the total corporate, publicly traded bond market. In 1987 and 1988 the public market supply of high-yield bonds averaged $31 billion. Industrial issuers principally comprise this market, rather than utility, transportation, or finance borrowers of capital. Since the industrial component of the domestic investment-grade corporate bond sector amounts to approximately $175 billion principal amount, the size of the public high-yield market now rivals that of the traditional, conservative, industrial high-grade investment universe.

A recent Salomon Brothers (1989) report on high-yield corporate bonds argued for their consideration as a legitimate asset class for asset allocation purposes by institutional investors. Defining high-yields as those nonconvertible corporates with bond credit ratings of Bal and lower by Moody's Investors Service, or BB+ and lower by Standard & Poor's, the report compared the rates of return and volatility to that of the U.S. equity market (S&P 500) and two investment-grade bond indices. Over the nine-year period 1980–88, the high-yield asset class as measured by Salomon Brothers' long-term high-yield index (LTHYI) outperformed the other two investment-grade fixed-income asset classes and came closest to the performance of the S&P 500. Moreover, the volatility of the high-yield asset declined over time.

Another recent study (Blume and Keim, 1989) arrived at a somewhat similar conclusion. Considering the eleven-year period 1977–87, the authors concluded that a portfolio of well-diversified low-grade bonds had no greater risk than a portfolio of high-grade bonds and that the historical return for the low grades exceeded that of the high grades; furthermore, low-grade bonds provide good diversification when used with other risky assets—owing to the less-than-perfect correlation with those assets.

Returns From Investing in High-Yield Debt

At the end of March 1989, on the average, high-yield bonds offered yields that were 4.5 percentage points higher than the Treasury yields. High-yield bonds performed well in 1988 based on total rates of return. While the S&P 500 index had a total return of 16.81% LTHYI had a slightly lower return of 16.11%. The corporate sector of the Salomon investment-grade bond index had a much lower return of 10.94%. In terms of risk as measured by the volatility or standard deviation of monthly returns in 1988, LTHYI had the lowest risk at 5.13%, while the S&P 500 had a risk of 9.64%. Considering a longer historical period of nine years, 1980–88, as shown in Table 2.4, LTHYI had an annual rate of return close to that of stocks with far less volatility. The income component of LTHYI, with its high return and very low volatility, is the reason for the superior performance of the high-yield security on a risk-return basis. Table 2.5 details the proportion of income return to total return for equity and fixed income assets. Moreover, the coefficients of correlation between LTHYI and the S&P 500 and between LTHYI and corporate high-grade bonds are low enough to consider using high-yield bonds as a distinct asset class in a well-diversified investment portfolio. The increasing correlation between LTHYI and the S&P 500 indicates the increasing similarity in return patterns of the two assets.

Blume and Keim (1989), with a low-grade bond index constructed from a combination of Drexel Burnham and Salomon Brothers indices corrected for survivor bias and extending the data back to 1977, came to the conclusion that low-grade bonds, owing to their low correlations with an equity index and other bond sectors (high-grade and government bonds), would prove to be an effective diversification vehicle for a portfolio consisting of equities and bonds. Additionally, they also found that the low-grade bonds were issued by smaller companies or firms with a high correlation with the small stock index of Ibbotson-Sinquefield. Interestingly, the compound annual return (over the period 1982–85) on the stocks of the low-grade bond issuers was found to be less than that for their bonds.

The lower total risk of the high-yield bond security relative to the high-grade bond could be explained as follows: (1) Owing to the high coupon rates, high-yield securities have short durations; thus, they are less sensitive to interest rate changes than the investment-grade bonds. To the extent the market environment was characterized by high interest rate volatility, junk bonds would have exhibited less variability than the investment-grade bonds. (2) Since the equity cushion protecting the high-yield bond is typically smaller than for the investment-grade bonds, the high-yield bond is more sensitive to fluctuations in the value of the issuing firm's assets. As a result the variability of junk bond returns is

Table 2.4
High-Yield Debt and Other Assets: Annual Compound Total Rates of Return and Volatility, 1980–88

Asset Class	1980–88		1985–88	
	Annual Rate of Return	Standard Deviation	Annual Rate of Return	Standard Deviation
S&P 500	16.09%	16.74%	17.78%	18.66%
LTHYI	14.03%	11.46%	14.68%	6.38%
Corp. BIG	12.57%	10.28%	13.06%	6.62%
Coefficient of Correlation between LTHYI & S&P 500 :	0.45		0.63	
Coefficient of Correlation between LTHYI & Corp. BIG :	0.85		0.57	

Note: LTHYI and Corp. BIG are Salomon Brothers Long Term High Yield Bond Index and the corporate sector of Broad Investment Grade Bond index, respectively; standard deviation is annualized from monthly return data.

Source: Salomon Brothers, February 1989.

more heavily influenced by sector, industry, and firm-specific factors than is the case with the investment-grade bonds. Much of this specific risk, however, is diversifiable in a large portfolio or index of junk bonds. These characteristics impart on junk bonds the elements of equity and, like common stocks, junk bond values would move in sympathy with the issuing firm's asset values. However, unlike common stocks, the upward movement is truncated for junk bonds beyond a certain point because of the callable feature of these bonds. If the issuing firm's creditworthiness improves dramatically, it will find it advantageous to call the bonds and refinance at a lower rate.

In the final analysis, investing in junk bonds is similar to a covered call option strategy with a long position in stocks and a short (written) position in the calls of that stock. If the stock declines, the short call position acts as the source of income owing to the premium received in writing the calls; if the stock appreciates, the stock's upside potential is

Table 2.5
Income Component of Annual Total Rates of Return, 1980–88

Asset Class	1980–88	1985–88
S&P 500	31%	24%
LTHYI	109%	95%
Corp. BIG	93%	81%

Source: Salomon Brothers, February 1989.

limited owing to the potential of the written call being exercised. Similarly, the junk bond's high current yield affords the investor some protection against the possibility that the firm's assets will decline in value. On the other hand, if the firm's value improves substantially, the firm will ultimately call the bonds away. This limits the upside potential.

Considering a different type of high-yield index constructed from estimated prices (so-called matrix prices), for the year ending in the first quarter of 1989, the high-yield corporate debt index (Merrill Lynch) had a return of 9.76% compared to an investment-grade corporate debt return of 7.08%. For the same period, high-yield convertible bonds (which have equity elements imbedded in them) returned 11.06% compared to the 10.06% by investment-grade convertibles. According to Altman (1989), high-yield junk bonds have consistently outperformed returns on risk-free and investment-grade fixed-income securities over the last decade, with average annual total returns of about 12%. He also states that a recent General Accounting Office-sponsored research study performed by Wharton Econometric Forecasting Associates concluded that, on a risk-adjusted basis, high-yield bonds ranked as one of the most profitable investments for thrifts, coming in second to credit card activities. On a cumulative basis, from 1980 to 1988, junk bonds yielded a compounded return of 208%, high-grade corporate bonds 156%, and long-term Treasury bonds 182%.[13] However, in years of declining interest rates, Treasury and high-grade corporate issues performed better because their prices rose far more than those of junk bonds.

Default Rate Experience of High-Yield Debt

Default risk due to inability of the issuer to make interest and principal payments is a real concern for buyers of high-yield debt. Bankruptcy filing by the issuer renders the reinstatement of interest and principal payments in doubt. Additionally, exchange offers (substitution of the defaulting series with a much less valuable bond series) permissible under the Securities Act of 1933 outside of the bankruptcy courts makes imprecise any estimation of principal loss incurred because of financial distress. Even so, what has been the best estimate of realized or experienced default rate on high-yield bonds? For the period 1978–88, the average yearly default rate was 1.86% per year. However, as Altman (1988) pointed out, the default rate does not measure the default loss. Investors generally recoup some value even on defaulted bonds. Historically, defaulted bonds have sold at an average rate of 40% of par value after default. This recovery rate has been 50% in the 1985–88 period. Accounting for this recovery, the average investor lost only 1.24% per year over the last 15 years, and 1.6% per year over the last four years.

Insights into the return potential of high-yield bonds could be obtained by considering them not as one single class of low-rated bonds but by their individual bond rating. By considering the default experience of different bond ratings (AAA through CCC) for the period 1971 through 1987, Altman (1988) constructed marginal mortality rates for cohorts of bonds year by year. For each bond rating he thus had an annual default rate for the first through tenth years after issuance. From these annual default rates the cumulative mortality rates were then computed. Based on historical performance over the period 1971–87, for AAA rated bonds, for example, the cumulative mortality rate at the end of five years after issuance was 0.00%, while that for BB was 1.84%, for B bonds 11.53%, and for CCC bonds 31.17%. Ten years after issuance, the cumulative default rates for the same bond rating classes were 0.13%, 6.64%, 31.91%, and not available for the CCC bonds. (Since then, new issues in this category were essentially nonexistent prior to 1982.) A word of caution: the longer term (ten years) mortality rates should be analyzed with caution when used as a predictor of future behavior of the market, since the years 1971–77 are the only ones contributing to the ten-year results, and so on. As a case in point, the surprisingly large cumulative default rate for B-rated bonds is a result of relatively small issue amounts throughout the 1970s.

To calculate the cumulative loss experience from investing in the bonds, the default rates for the various bond rating classes will have to be adjusted by their default recovery rates—that is, the actual amount recovered by selling the defaulted bond. Altman (1988) found the average recovery rate for all classes combined was about 40%. Integrating the default and recovery concepts, if the performances of the debt classes were evaluated as realized return spreads over risk-free government bonds, Altman (1988) found that for the first three years after issuance, the lower the bond rating the higher the net return spread, with B-rated bonds doing the best. Overall, over the ten-year horizon, BB-rated bonds seemed to have performed the best. However, when market conditions during the period October 1987 to early 1988 are considered, the B-rated bonds seemed to dominate all the other classes. Also, for all holding periods, all bond types do well and have positive spreads over Treasuries.

Jerome Fons (1987) developed a risk-neutral model of the expected probability of default for low-grade bonds (below BBB- or Baa3) as a function of the required risk premium over default-free bonds. An expected model-based default rate on the high-yield issues was then estimated. Using data covering the period January 1980 through December 1985, he then compared the actual default experience of low-rated debt with the model estimated default rate. Such a comparison recognizes the fact that measured, ex-post holding period returns are poor indicators of expected default rates. He found that the default rates implied in corporate bond returns exceed those experienced. He concluded that holders of well-diversified portfolios of low-rated corporate bonds appear to be rewarded for bearing default risk. An alternative model of expected default rates also yielded similar results. Additionally, among the macroeconomic factors that could influence the default premium, he found deviations from inflation expectations (inflation surprise) to have the greatest influence.

A recent report by Morgan Stanley (1989) concluded that the spreads between high-yield bonds and ten-year U.S. Treasuries have been adequate and that investor expectation of any burgeoning recession and the consequent increased risk of default is reflected in the widening spread. Figure 2.1 charts the spread between a high-yield bond composite and ten-year U.S. Treasuries for the period May 1986–March 1989 with purported reasons identifying major changes in the yield spread.

A more recent unpublished study by Harvard University professor Paul Asquith and two colleagues[14] seemed to suggest that a portfolio of all the junk bonds issued in 1977 and 1978 would, by November 1, 1988, have experienced a default rate of more than 34%. The Harvard study suggested that of the junk bonds issued from 1979 through 1983, between 19% and 26% had defaulted by November 1988. Default rates for junk bonds issued between 1984 and 1986 ranged from 4% to 9% by November 1988. The study also seems to have found that a significant portion of junk bonds in their early years are subject to exchange offers where the bonds are swapped for other securities; a large fraction of these offers resulted in defaults. The Harvard study suggested that measuring default rates as a ratio of the annual default value to the value of total outstanding high-yield issues masks or understates the true default rate, since (1) the default rate for a typical bond issue is low in the initial years but rises over time, and (2) the explosive growth in new issues results in the overall market being dominated by recently issued bonds

Figure 2.1
High-Yield Bond Spread, May 1986–March 1989; High-Yield Composite versus 10-Year U.S. Treasuries

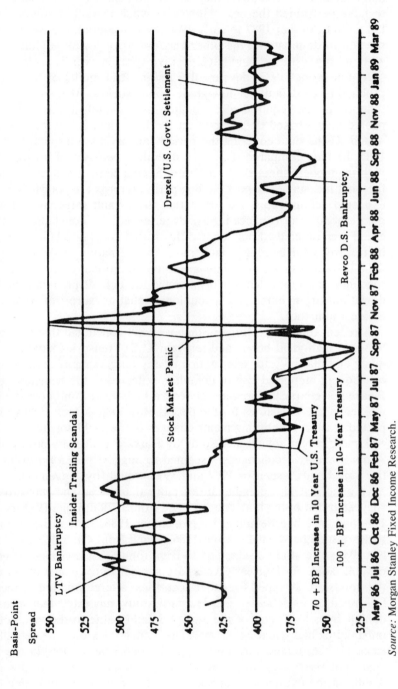

Source: Morgan Stanley Fixed Income Research.

40

with low default rates. These results, though, are not radically different from the default rates discussed above in the context of the Altman (1988) marginal mortality study.

The studies on default rates suggest the following caution: unless the high-yield portfolio is essentially made of well-diversified, new issues with an investment horizon extending over a period of one or two years, the low annual default rate of about 2% would be an underestimate of the actual default experience. Moreover, the importance of good research and meticulous scrutiny to avoid especially risky issues cannot be overemphasized for a portfolio with a long investment horizon.

Finally, the firm-specific risk in a high-yield portfolio is likely to be much larger than in an investment-grade bond portfolio. This is clear from an analysis of the defaulted bond statistics over the period 1980–88. The percent of total defaulted bonds in any given year that is accounted for by the largest issuer varied from 82% in 1980 to a low of 27% in 1988 with an average of 43.8% (not counting Texaco, which was responsible for 82% of the defaulted bonds in 1987) and 48.9% including Texaco in the 1987 default experience. This requires expense of substantial effort by the portfolio manager in understanding the individual business characteristics of each debt issuer and a close scrutiny of the bond covenants specific to each issue.

High-Yield Debt, Leveraged Buyouts, and Corporate Takeovers

Seasoned senior public debtholders (i.e., existing bondholders) of investment-grade issuers face considerable price drops and default risk when the firm undertakes capital restructuring that favors the shareholders at the expense of the preexisting bondholders. Bondholders of companies such as Allied Stores, American Standard, Federated Department Stores, Fruehauf, and USG suffered significant price and severe credit deterioration following leveraged restructurings of these companies' balance sheets. For Federated Department Stores, the drop for senior debt was from AA- to B. Leveraged buyout is the acquisition of the stock or assets of an existing entity by an investor group, with the funds for the acquisition provided principally in the form of long-term borrowings. The investment-grade bonds issued by RJR Nabisco dropped a dizzying 20% after management proposed the largest LBO in history. When Fruehauf, once the General Motors of truck trailers and one of the 200 largest industrial concerns in the United States, informed the Securities and Exchange Commission (SEC) in January 1989 of its inability to remain solvent by year end and began dismembering the firm on March 28, 1989, it acquired the dubious distinction of becoming the biggest LBO to date to go bankrupt.

If severe price erosion is the risk faced by existing bondholders of the

Table 2.6
Recent Bond Yields of Some High-Risk Buyout Companies

Company	Transaction Date	Bond Yield
Fruehauf Corp.	December 1986	18%–plus
Leasway Transportation	June 1987	17%
Morse Shoe Inc.	July 1987	20%–plus
Papercraft Corp.	1985	19%–plus
Gillett Holdings	December 1987	17.5%
Synthetic Industries	December 1986	18%
Trans World Airlines	October 1988	22%
Metropolitan Broadcasting	November 1986	17%
Allied Stores Corp.	December 1986	17%
Southland Corp.	December 1987	18.5%*

Note: Rates given are yield to maturity for junior bonds. Bonds that don't currently pay interest, such as zero–coupon bonds, are noted with an asterisk. Such yields are normally higher than coupon-paying bonds.

Source: *The Wall Street Journal*, December 5, 1988.

once-blue-chip companies, the same security, after the fall, now offers potential for very high returns. Owing to the negative pledge clauses (that is, limitations on the granting of liens on unpledged assets unless the covenanted debt is equally and ratably secured) in the covenants of the existing bonds with senior status, these continue to be secured on a *pari passu* basis with the companies' other senior lenders (bank loans, etc). Thus the favorable collateral status and treatment of secured obligations in bankruptcy law would compensate, to some extent, the decline in credit ratings and deterioration of historical yield spreads. These "fallen angels," besides offering wider spreads than are available from investment-grade paper, also avoid the "event risk," (a further significant decline in credit ratings due to capital restructuring, takeover, or LBO) that exist at many industrial-grade issuers. An indication of the potential for high returns from investment in risky corporate bonds is shown in Table 2.6. These were the bond yields available on those corporate bonds as of December 1988. The level of risk is also significantly high. Fruehauf, for instance, indicated on March 29, 1989, that by year end it is likely to be insolvent.

Public policy debates concerning high-yield bonds have tended to attribute the current perceived market volatility and precariousness of the financial system to these junk bonds. The very unsavory moniker "junk bonds" attached to high-yield debt is indicative of the public perception of that financial instrument. Let us consider the facts. According to Perry and Taggart (1988), junk bond issues accounted for only 6% of the total credit market debt that companies raised during the period 1977–86. How much of the mergers and acquisition activity did junk bonds finance? According to the same study, approximately 40% of the public junk bond issues related to the mergers and acquisition activities during the 1980s. Assuming the size of the high-yield market to be $180 billion (at the end of 1988), mergers and acquisition-related junk bonds amounted to $72 billion. According to Goldman Sachs (1989), total mergers and acquisition activity over the period 1982–87 was $511 billion. Thus, junk bonds financed approximately 14% of the mergers and acquisition activity during 1982–87. Perry and Taggart (1988) had estimated junk bond financing of the mergers and acquisition activity to be 7.8% in 1986, 4.3% in 1985, and 2.6% in 1984. Thus bank loans and equity exchanges are a far bigger source of merger financing than junk bonds.

How about junk bonds and leveraged buyouts? Again, Goldman Sachs (1989) estimated that roughly 75% of $420 billion equity reduction (capital restructuring) since 1982 was debt financed. Also, of all the restructurings involving the substitution of debt for equity capital in the 1982–88 period, LBOs represented a relatively small 20%. Thus LBO-related debt during the period 1982–88 is roughly $63 billion. As a fraction of the total LBO activity amounting to $88 billion during 1982–88, debt represents a high of 72%. LBOs are, in general, highly debt intensive. Even so, according to Salomon Brothers (1988), LBO-related high-yield debt as a fraction of the total principal amount of high-yield new issuance rose from only 25.3% in 1986 to 34.2% in 1988. LBOs, as the label connotes, are largely financed through debt. The ideal junk bond issuer is a firm that has a total market value that is largely attributable to assets in place. Such a firm is likely to have a greater debt capacity than one whose market value is based on assessment of prospective future investments. Thus a firm with a mature business that generates a high but relatively steady level of cash flows or a young firm that has cleared the product and market development hurdles and is positioned for a major expansion have been ideal candidates for recent LBOs. Goldman Sachs (1989) also found that some 60% (excluding the mammoth $25 billion RJR Nabisco LBO) of the industrial LBOs over the period 1982–88 were in the stable, noncyclical industries.

Appendix 2 outlines the typical elements that make a firm an attractive candidate for LBO. The appendix also contains a description of a typical schedule of the process that takes place in a successful transformation of a public firm into an LBO.

Typical High-Yield Bond Investors

By 1987, insurance companies bought 30% of the junk bonds, mutual fund money managers bought another 30%, pension funds 15%, while foreign investors, individuals, S&Ls, and corporations accounted for the remaining 25%. Many insurance companies and pension funds view junk bonds as a replacement for the stocks of companies that were taken over or underwent an LBO. According to Drexel Burnham the fastest-growing group of investors in the junk bond market is foreigners whose market share is well over 5%. Japanese institutions, ranging from corporations with excess cash and an appetite for *zaitech* to insurance and leasing companies, are said to be buying bonds at the rate of $1 billion a month.

In the United States, federal regulations prohibit commercial banks from investing in junk bonds, although the bonds can be bought by bank holding companies. However, the banks have not been idle bystanders watching the high-yield debt market go past them. According to Standard & Poor's, some big banks may have devoted as much as 40% of their U.S. business lending to debt-financed corporate buyouts. The hefty fees associated with financing buyouts is an important reason in the banks' appetites for such loans. As a rule, the annual interest rate on senior debt in buyouts is priced at 2 to 2.5 percentage points over LIBOR (London Interbank Offered Rate) and carries fees that typically run about 2% of the loan amount. Rates and fees on more conventional corporate loans usually are considerably less. For instance, in the $25 billion RJR Nabisco buyout deal, some 200 banks will share $325 million in agent and facility fees for providing $14.5 billion in senior debt. In addition, they will receive about $73 million in annual commitment fees. Had the deal fallen through, the banks would have received $150 million in termination fees.

Buyout portfolios on the books of the banks are only a fraction of the buyout loan volume they arrange. This is because they sell out a major portion of their buyout lending to other foreign and domestic investors, including insurance companies, pension funds, foreign banks, and thrifts. At the end of 1988, the ten major banks held a total of $19 billion in senior debt to buyouts—a fraction, about 20%, of the volume of senior buyout debt arranged by them. Table 2.7 lists some of the major bank lenders to LBOs and their exposure to this type of asset in their portfolios.

An unwelcome side effect of the widening high-yield debt market is its impact on the corporate high-grade bond market. Suddenly, the investors in the blue chip corporations are made aware of the "event risk" inherent in any company's debt issues. In the post-RJR Nabisco LBO era no corporation appears to be immune to a leveraged takeover—hostile or friendly. High-grade bonds are converted into junk bonds

Table 2.7
Major Bank Lenders to LBOs

Bank	LBO portfolio (Billions)	LBO loans underwritten[*]	Percent retained after syndication[*]	LBO loans' share of total portfolio[*]
Citicorp	$4.0	Very High	Moderate	High
Wells Fargo	$3.0	High	High	Very High
Bankers Trust	$2.7	Very High	Moderate to HIgh	Very High
Security Pacific	$2.4	High	Moderate	High
Manufacturers Hanover	$1.5-2.0	Very High	Moderate	High
Bank America	$1.3	Moderate	Moderate	Moderate
Chase Manhattan	$1.25	Moderate	Moderate	Moderate
First Chicago	$1.2	High	Moderate	High
Continental Illinois	$0.927	Moderate	Moderate	Moderate
J.P.Morgan	$0.7-0.8	High	Moderate	Moderate
Chemical	NA	High	Moderate	High

<u>Note:</u> [*] Descriptions reflect size of LBO portfolio relative to peers and to a company's domestic commercial and industrial loan portfolio. The descriptions are from a Standard & Poor's report as published in *The Wall Street Journal*, December 5, 1988.

Source: The Wall Street Journal, December 5 and 13, 1988.

---

overnight after the leveraged bid is announced. The debt of a potential takeover target now trades some 1.5 percentage points above the level suggested by its blue chip rating. RJR investment-grade bond prices dropped 20% after management proposed the largest LBO in history. Federated Department Stores' senior debt went from AA to B junk after Campeau's debt-financed takeover. When R.H. Macy proposed its $3.6 billion LBO in 1985, its stock jumped by $16 a share while the price of its debt notes fell more than three points. Bondholders have responded by insisting on inclusion of protective covenants by the issuing companies that limit losses in any future capital restructuring. These are the so-called poison puts that give the bondholders the right to sell their bonds back to the company at face value if a restructuring lowers their rating below investment grade. Another response has been the increased activism of bondholder associations that now insist on tighter protective covenants against cash outflows along with cash compensation in case of capital restructuring. Some have pursued legal actions against the management to recover their initial bond investments. Metlife and ITT's Hartford Insurance are two examples of corporate bond investors who have sought legal redressals from the credit erosion resulting from leveraged takeover proposals from the management of the companies. Such activism by the senior debtholders of the once-blue chip firms would tend to make the high-yield debt of the LBO more risky due to less equity and collateral covering the risky debt.

Some institutional investors in LBO partnerships have begun reassessing the risk of such investments in the wake of the mega RJR Nabisco LBO. The very demand for junk bonds by investors may have led to the soaring buyout prices highlighted by the record bidding for RJR Nabisco. Such fears have led to caution and perhaps curbing of future commitments to LBO partnerships by pension funds, insurance companies, and endowments. Even so, estimates of current commitments by institutional investors to partnerships dedicated to investments in LBOs put the figure at $25 billion. At the typical LBO debt to equity ratio of 9 to 1, the $25 billion of LBO equity could potentially create $225 billion more of high-yield debt and LBO loans. However, the increasing reluctance of LBO lenders (banks) and, possibly, investors in high-yield debt could raise the equity component needed to carry out an LBO in the future and thus lower somewhat the potential size of the LBO debt market.

How to Invest in Junk Bonds

Altman (1987) estimated that at the end of 1986 there were 55 open-end mutual funds investing in high-current-yield corporate debt, with total net assets of $25.9 billion. By April 1989, according to Lipper Analytical Services, there were 119 junk bond funds with a total of nearly $47 billion in assets, up 20% from 1988.[15] The rapid growth in junk bond funds is an indication of its popularity to the retail (noninstitutional) investor. It is also possible that some corporate-bond funds, owing to the wide latitude allowed to their portfolio managers in their quest for larger and larger yield pick-up, ended up investing in high-yield bonds.

Examples of some corporate bond funds with the percentage of their net assets invested in junk bonds at the end of 1988 are: Strong Income Fund with 90% of its assets in junk bonds, National Bond Fund with 81%, Nicholas Income Fund with 40%, American Capital Corporation Bond Fund with 36%, CIGNA Income Fund with 11%, and United Bond Fund with 10%.[16] A common reason cited by the corporate bond fund managers to explain their investments in junk bonds is the increasing frequency of leveraged takeovers and mergers of the once-blue chip firms. Such leveraged mergers result in quality erosion of the once-high-grade bonds to high-yield debt. These are the so-called fallen angels. Thus buying high-yield bonds is preferred over possessing high-grade bonds that become low-grade while in possession. There are of course bond funds with explicit mandates to invest in high-yield securities. The prospectuses of such funds make clear their intention to invest in high-yield bonds. Examples of such funds are the Keystone B4 High-Yield Fund and the Alliance High Yield Fund, among others.

Junk bonds are generally considered inappropriate for the individual investor. Sophisticated institutional investors and professional money managers who have the resources to analyze and assess the default characteristics of high-yield bonds and who are able to reduce risk due to holding a diversified portfolio are the "natural" investors in junk bonds. Still, with yields that promise some of the highest returns that investors can earn, individuals do find junk bonds attractive as an investment vehicle. Here are some commonsensical safeguards that junk bond investors (individuals) ought to take:

1. Since adequate diversification can be achieved only with a portfolio of 10 to 20 bonds at a cost of $100,000 or more, the smaller investor with more modest sums to invest ought to think of a managed mutual fund.

2. Junk bond holdings ought to be diversified by investing in unrelated categories of issuers. The three types of junk bonds are the so-called fallen angels (bonds when originally issued were blue chip that have since fallen or downgraded to low grade), emerging growth company issues, and the high-yield debt issued by companies undergoing capital restructuring.

3. Only liquid and publicly listed bonds ought to be bought. Liquidity (i.e., bond issues with outstanding amounts exceeding $100 million) ensures that selling the bond would not take unduly long while public listing of the bond on stock exchanges enables easy acquisition of price and yield information to monitor the portfolio.

4. Unusually high yields could indicate unusually high risk. Avoid buying high-yield bonds in the higher end of the range of yields unless very detailed analysis based on hard-to-get information suggests that the market may have overestimated the potential default rate (hence, underpriced the issue) of the bond.

5. Buy bonds with protective covenants—the provisions in the bond prospectus that protect bondholders from adverse outcome. An institutional bond investor in private placements can insist on certain ironclad guarantees in the event of an adverse outcome like leveraged capital restructuring that results in increased debt. For the individual investor in publicly traded bonds the covenants are the only legal shield that offers protection. The common protective covenants relate to the suspension of dividends or common stock repurchase by the firm when earnings are inadequate; the promise to maintain positive net worth by reducing debt (buy back bonds) when the equity component of

the balance sheet is whittled away through losses; the promise not to enervate the company through merger or sale of assets thus leaving a shell to service the debts.

ARE RETURNS TO STOCKHOLDERS IN BANKRUPT FIRMS "EXCESSIVE"?

The objective of this research is twofold: to test the efficiency of the market for Chapter 11 stocks by determining if excess risk-adjusted returns were earned by investors purchasing these equities after the companies had filed for bankruptcy, and to test whether risk itself changes over time for these firms. In Chapter 5 we develop a logit model that could be used to identify factors that will predict successful reorganization of firms filing for bankruptcy.

While past studies concentrated on determining how the market reacts to a bankruptcy announcement or how an investor can predict bankruptcy, this study looks at the after-filing returns and risk characteristics of Chapter 11 firms and determines what changes occurred in the riskiness of the firms' pre- and post-bankruptcy filing and reorganization. We use intervention analysis, as well as the traditional cumulative average residual analysis approach when testing for the excess return (return in excess of the market-related return). To account for the problem of infrequent trading in these securities we calculate excess returns using the Dimson method (see Dimson, 1979).

Altman (1969a) developed a model to quantify the risk/return performance of a bankrupt firm's stocks. He then empirically tested the model with data taken from the time period 1941–65. Altman's results showed that common shareholders of a bankrupt firm tended to earn as much return as all other equityholders of New York Stock Exchange stock, if the reorganized firm survived for at least five years after its filing date. A problem with Altman's study is that the rates of return for the bankrupt sample were risk-adjusted, assuming constancy of systematic (market) risk of the firms. Aharony et al. (1980) did one of the few studies that addressed the question of risk changes for firms that filed under Chapter X. They showed that the total risk of a firm's returns (measured by the variance of returns) and its unsystematic risk component showed a dramatic increase when compared to similar successful firms. Their analysis, however, did not extend beyond the filing dates of the sampled firms. All of the sampled firms had filed for bankruptcy under the old Chapter X, thus the time period of study ended in 1978. The sample for our study, on the other hand, includes those firms that filed Chapter 11 petitions for reorganizations after the new law became effective on October 1, 1979, and survived for at least a year after filing.

Research Design

Several assumptions were made regarding the treatment of Chapter 11 firms in this study. The first was that a bankruptcy announcement effect existed and was properly incorporated into the Chapter 11 firms' stock prices. Supporting documentation for this assumption comes from Altman (1969b), Aharony et al. (1980), Altman and Brenner (1981), and Clark and Weinstein (1983). Using cumulative average residual analysis, their studies showed that prior to filing (under the old law), the market for bankrupt stocks behaved efficiently. The second assumption made in this study was that Chapter 11 firms were considered to be different firms after filing. Viewing these firms as new entities provided a way to test for any abnormal returns that existed after filing and for risk changes pre- to post-filing. The reasons for viewing firms from this perspective were:

1. When firms sought protection from creditors under Chapter 11, they were essentially asking the courts for permission to start over as new businesses.
2. The law gave these firms time to reorganize their operations, financial structures, and corporate policies, without the interference of unpaid creditors demanding compensation.
3. Many financially distressed firms emerged from reorganization proceedings smaller, having divested themselves of unprofitable divisions or subsidiaries, and with healthy balance sheets.
4. Finally, it can be argued that Chapter 11 firms have quite different objectives, financial structures, and policy decisions than before filing.

Weston (1977) supported the treatment of Chapter 11 firms in this manner, but evidence also comes from actual reorganization cases. After filing, many Chapter 11 firms immediately begin to sell off unprofitable divisions, to close down excess capacity, and to hire turn-around specialists with reputations for bringing firms out of reorganization. An example of a company that employed this strategy is Wickes of Santa Monica, California. Wickes, a diversified building materials retailer, filed for Chapter 11 protection in April 1982 with $2 billion worth of liabilities and $2 billion in assets. Wickes brought in a turn-around specialist to serve as its new chairman and president. After filing, Wickes sold its agricultural unit, closed down or sold 103 of its 3,000 stores, and cut the staff by 10%. Another Chapter 11 firm, Lionel, followed a similar plan and thus was able to start over as a new firm.[17]

Data

A sample of 50 firms was selected from a list of the approximately 200 firms that filed for Chapter 11 between October 1, 1979, and December

31, 1983. This list was obtained from the Corporate Reorganization Department of the SEC. We chose sample companies from the population of Chapter 11 firms using the following criteria: (1) monthly and daily return or price data were available publicly; (2) financial information on a firm was obtainable from *Moody's Industrial Manuals* just prior to filing. Monthly return data for the sample were obtained for the time period before filing from the Center for Research on Security Prices (CRSP) tapes. Daily return data were also obtained from the CRSP tapes for 24 firms. If a sample stock traded over-the-counter (OTC) before filing, monthly and daily price quotes were collected from Standard & Poor's Daily OTC Stock Price Record. These prices were converted into stock returns as follows:

$$R_{j,t} = \frac{P_{j,t} - P_{j,t-1} + D_{j,t}}{P_{j,t-1}} \tag{1}$$

where
$R_{j,t}$ = the holding period return for stock j from time t_{-1} to t
$P_{j,t}$ = the price of stock j at time t
$P_{j,t-1}$ = the price of stock j at time t_{-1}
$D_{j,t}$ = the dividend paid on the stock during the time t_{-1} to t

Because we were concerned only with the impact of a Chapter 11 filing on a firm's risk and return measures around the actual date of filing, we limited pre-filing stock return data to a period beginning two years before filing. Although some studies have shown that firms approaching bankruptcy experience changes in their stock returns up to five years before filing, Altman (1969) shows that the final drop in price occurs within a month of filing. In fact, his evidence indicates that the market is surprised by the bankruptcy announcement, because the price drops by an additional 30 to 50% right before filing. Thus two years of return data before filing would allow us to test for any changes in risk and return measures after filing. Depending on the type of data available, we divided the sample into three groups:

1. Group 1 consisted of 24 firms for which daily return or price data were available after filing and for the two years before filing. After-filing data were available until the firm was reorganized, merged into another firm, was liquidated, or through December 31, 1983.

2. Group 2 had end-of-the-month return or price data obtainable for the same time periods as Group 1 and consisted of all 50 firms.

3. Group 3 consisted of 11 firms from Group 1. The firms chosen had reorganized or liquidated by December 31, 1982.

For testing purposes, a portfolio of Chapter 11 firms was formed that included all the firms in Group 1. Because each firm had a different filing date, we employed a method used by Aharony et al. (1980) to form the time series of portfolio returns. Using the filing date as the beginning time for each firm, we calculated an average portfolio return by summing all the filing date returns of each firm. We then matched other daily returns by subtracting and adding days from the filing date to form a time series of portfolio returns. Figure 2.2 shows schematically what this procedure looks like.

Figure 2.2
Time Sequence of Returns

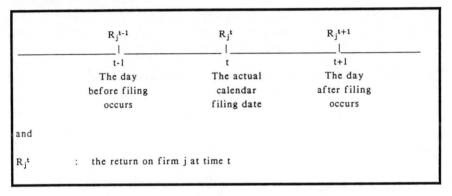

The portfolio return R_p^t for a specific time t was calculated such that

$$R_p^t = \frac{\sum_{j=1}^{n} R_j^t}{n} \qquad (2)$$

where n = number of firms

Collecting postfiling data for these firms was difficult. All but three of the companies that were listed on the New York Exchange before filing had trading suspended by the exchange. Investors then began trading these stocks on the Pacific Stock Exchange, or, in some cases, dealers traded the stocks over-the-counter. Daily price data for those stocks trading on the Pacific Exchange after their companies had filed for Chapter 11 protection were collected from daily editions of *The Wall Street Journal,* while daily price data for stocks trading over-the-counter were collected from Standard & Poor's Daily OTC Stock Price Record. For some companies only monthly stock price data were available. These were retrieved from the Pink Sheet Summaries provided by Merrill, Lynch.

Method of Analysis

Unlike some previous studies in this area, we wish to explicitly model the variation in systematic risk (market-related risk) that a bankrupt firm is expected to have in the pre- and post-bankruptcy periods. For this reason, we will perform the analysis two ways: using the more traditional cumulative average residual analysis and the more complex intervention analysis that recognizes the variation in the systematic risk of the firm over the post-bankruptcy period.

Cumulative Average Residual. The most common research methodology used in event studies is the cumulative average residual analysis (CAR). Fama et al. (1969) wrote the seminal article on the topic. They used the existence of non-zero cumulative average residuals as a test for the presence of abnormal returns for investors who purchased the common stocks of firms that had been split. An "abnormal return" is the difference between the actual return and the return estimated by a model. For instance, if the model used to estimate the return is the Capital Asset Pricing Model (CAPM) then abnormal return will be:

$$AR_{jt} = R_{jt} - E(R_{jt}/\hat{\beta}_{jt}) \tag{3}$$

where the estimated return will be given by the CAPM:

$$E(R_{jt}) = R_{ft} + (R_{mt} - R_{ft})\hat{\beta}_j \tag{4}$$

where
R_{ft} = Actual Risk-free rate
R_{mt} = Actual Market return
$\hat{\beta}_j$ = Estimated market beta for stock j

The usual technique is to estimate AR_{jt} over an interval surrounding the economic event of interest. For a given time period t, the average abnormal return, AR_t, for a portfolio of randomly chosen stocks is obtained by averaging the abnormal returns across firms. Thus, at time t, the average abnormal return is

$$AR_t = \frac{\sum_{j=1}^{N} AR_{jt}}{N} \tag{5}$$

where
N = the number of stocks in the portfolio

The cumulative average residual or abnormal return is the sum of the average abnormal return over all periods from the start of the data ($t=1$) to the current period t.

$$CAR_t = \sum_{t=1}^{t} AR_t \tag{6}$$

The CAR_t at time t shows the cumulative effects of the wanderings of the actual returns of the common stocks from their expected returns as measured by the CAPM model. Since the time of this seminal article, many researchers have used cumulative average residual analysis to determine how certain events affect the stock returns of firms and if investors purchasing these stocks after the events had occurred could earn abnormal returns. These authors were testing to see if the market incorporated the news of certain events into their assessments of the prices of the affected stocks before and after the events occurred. Since one of the objectives of this analysis is to determine if the market for the common stocks of reorganizing firms behaved efficiently around the time of the filing, the sample firms were tested for abnormal performance using cumulative average residual analysis.

Since 1969, many researchers have questioned the use of cumulative average residual analysis as a way of determining if abnormal returns can be earned by investors. Sunder (1973) believed that the technique falsely indicated that abnormal returns had occurred when in fact what really happened was that the risk of the firm changed because of the occurrence of a specific event. He stated that in the presence of changes in risk the estimated abnormal returns on stocks are dependent on the time series data used for the estimation of relative risk. Brown and Warner (1980) studied various methodologies for measuring abnormal performance. Using simulation on monthly data, they generated abnormal performance of different levels and tested to see which methodology correctly specified that significant abnormal return performance occurred in the data. With regard to cumulative average residual analysis, they found that if the exact month of the event could be pinpointed, then the technique correctly indicated the presence of abnormal returns, but that the level of those abnormal returns was not correctly specified.

Brown and Warner also found that the market model[18] was a very good one to use when estimating abnormal return performance, and that the t-test was the best statistical test to use when determining if the market model residuals are significantly different from zero, or if abnormal returns exist. They found that the power of the t-test to correctly reject the null hypothesis of no abnormal returns increased as the magnitude of the abnormal return performance increased. In summary, although we used the cumulative average residual technique to determine if abnormal performance was evident after filing, Box and Tiao's (1975) intervention analysis was also used as changes in risk over time can be incorporated in their model.

*Intervention Analysis.*Box and Tiao (1975) developed a methodology, called intervention analysis, that can be applied to event studies. Larcker, Gordon, and Pinches (1980) are responsible for adapting the Box and Tiao analysis to stock price data. There are two approaches that can be used to apply the following intervention model to time series data:

$$Z_t = f(w,d,a) \tag{7}$$

where
Z_t = the time series variable to be modeled and predicted
w = all exogenous variables
d = intervention variables
a = noise modeled with an ARIMA (Autoregressive Integrated Moving Average) process

The first approach is to develop estimates of a noise model using the time series observations (Z_t) prior to the event date or intervention point. These estimates are then tested to see if the same process, as specified by the model, will generate the time series of Z_ts after an event date. If the noise model estimates are not significantly different before and after an event date, then least squares regression is employed to estimate the values of the exogenous variables and the coefficients of the intervention variables. The estimated coefficients of the intervention variables are evaluated in the same manner as other regression coefficients.

The second approach is to estimate the noise model, the coefficients of the exogenous variables, and the intervention variables simultaneously using nonlinear regression. Either method gives the same intervention parameters, as long as the noise model parameters remain constant after the intervention or event date. When testing stock return data for abnormal performance, Larcker et al. (1980) suggest that the following model be applied to the time series data:

$$R_{jt} = \beta_1 R_{mt} I_1 + \beta_2 R_{mt} I_2 + \beta_3 R_{mt} I_3 + E_1 I_1 + E_2 I_2 + \frac{\theta(B)}{(1-B)^d \phi(B)} \alpha_t \tag{8}$$

where
R_{jt} = the return on the stock of firm j at time t
β_1,β_2,β_3 = systematic risk estimates for periods 1, 2, and 3 (these are polynomials in the backward shift operator, B, which is explained below)
R_{mt} = the return on the market portfolio at time t
I_1,I_2,I_3 = dummy variables equal to zero or 1 such that:

I_n = 1 for period n where n = 1, 2, or 3; 0 otherwise

E_1, E_2 = estimates of abnormal stock return performance for periods 1 and 2; when E_1 and E_2 are not significantly different from zero then no abnormal return performance exists during the period

$$\frac{\theta(B)}{(1-B)^d \phi(B)} \alpha_t = \text{the noise model estimates of the time series, } R_{jt}$$

where

B = Backward shift operator such that $Bz_t = z_{t-1}$ and $B^k z_t = z_{t-k}$

$\theta(B)$ and $\phi(B)$ = polynomials in B, defined as

$\phi(B)$ = $1 - \phi_1 B - \ldots - \phi_p B^p$

$\theta(B)$ = $1 - \theta_1 B - \ldots - \theta_p B^p$

This equation, when applied to a time series of stock return data, allows for changes in β_j to occur over time. This procedure is more powerful for detecting abnormal return performance than CAR analysis. In addition, not only are the estimates of risk allowed to change over time, but the noise model removes any autoregressive or moving average behavior that exists in the time series of stock return data. Any firm-specific risk that exists in the return data is modeled and does not, therefore, affect parameter estimation.

Methodological Issues

When applying cumulative average residual analysis, it is assumed that all firms in a portfolio exhibit the same return pattern on the days preceding and following the event date. For Chapter 11 firms, this is not true. (Chapter 6 will address this issue.) Calculating systematic risk estimates is also troublesome. Using the market model to estimate systematic risk assumes that the market for the stocks is efficient and that the stocks are, therefore, traded frequently. Even for Chapter 11 firms where daily price data are available, infrequent trading can occur. The price of the stock may not change for a few days or a week, resulting in consecutive returns being equal to zero. To correct for this bias in the systematic risk estimates we used a method presented by Dimson (1979). When shares are traded infrequently, systematic risk (or beta) estimates are often severely biased. Using the leading and lagging independent and dependent regression variables (market index returns), significant systematic risk estimates can be computed. Infrequent trading often results in regression parameters not being significantly different from zero.

Using Larcker et al. event methodology, we were also able to adjust for changes in systematic risk for firms across time. Two approaches were found to be necessary. First, Box and Tiao indicate that to use

Table 2.8
Estimates of Portfolio Systematic Risk

	β_I	Standard Deviation	T- Ratio	Degrees of Freedom
Before	1.025	0.2870	3.57	497
After	2.255	1.567	1.44	230

intervention analysis effectively the stochastic process driving a time series of data must remain constant over time. For each Group 3 firm, we
estimated the noise ARIMA model for the time period of two years preceding the filing date. Then using these significant parameters we used
equation 3 to compute the abnormal returns after filing. In addition we
estimated the ARIMA noise model for three different periods (before
filing, during reorganization, and after reorganization) and again tested
for the presence of abnormal returns. At this point we were interested
in seeing if the stochastic process generating these stock returns was
constant over time and, if not, then at what point or points did it change
for each firm.

Analysis and Results

The results indicate that for the portfolio of Group I firms (24 firms)
the systematic risk estimates increased after filing. Table 2.8 shows that
the average beta before filing was statistically significant at the 95% level
of confidence and equal to 1.025 while after filing the average beta increased to 2.255 and was significant at the 90% level of confidence. Figure 2.3 shows a plot of the cumulative average residuals over time and
indicates that the abnormal returns could be earned within 22 days of
filing. This means that the actual return is greater than the expected
return, which was risk-adjusted with the before-filing beta. Since the after-
filing beta is significantly higher than the before-filing beta, it is possible
that abnormal returns did not occur but that the portfolio's actual returns were higher than expected because the risk increased. Investors
need to be compensated for the increase in risk due to the uncertainties
of Chapter 11 filing.

Table 2.9 presents the results of intervention analysis on Group 3 firms.
The ARIMA model, specified in the last column of the table, was fit to
the prefiling data of each firm and was statistically significant at the .05
level at that time. When the model was fit to the entire data series (including the post-bankruptcy period), the significance of the ARIMA models

Figure 2.3
Cumulative Average Residuals

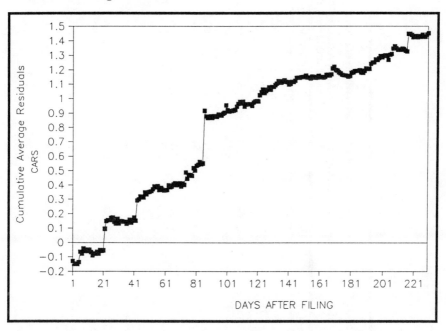

changed for some firms. Adding systematic risk parameter estimates and abnormal performance measures changed the significance of the ex-post model.

The results of our analyses indicate that the market return does not seem to provide a good explanatory variable for describing the behavior of a reorganizing firm's return series. Only seven out of thirty estimates were significantly different from zero at the .05 level. Even incorporating the Dimson correction technique (for infrequent trading) did not improve the significance of our systematic risk estimates. Although this technique corrected for changes in systematic risk across time, it is difficult to determine if the estimates did change since they for the most part were not significantly different than zero. The results of the tests for abnormal performance were also inconclusive. Only one firm had positive significant abnormal return performance before and after filing. Only three firms out of the eleven had exhibited abnormal return performances after filing. Given that the beta estimates were unreliable, it is difficult to draw any conclusions concerning abnormal performance of the stocks if investors purchased the securities after the firms filed.

In conclusion, it appears that the stock behavior of Chapter 11 firms can not be tested using market model analysis even though the analysis

Table 2.9
Results of Intervention Analysis: Group 3 Firms

Firm	Constant	Systematic Risk Estimates (T-statistics are given within brackets)			Abnormal Performance (T-statistics are given within brackets)		ARIMA Noise Model that was significant before filing	
		$F_1(B)$	$F_2(B)$	$F_3(B)$	E_1	E_2	ARIMA Parameters	
Arctic Enter-prises	6.5E-3 (2.44)*	0.828 (3.69)*	0.118@ (0.53)	0.378 (1.07)	-.01 (-3.03)*	-2.4E-3 (-0.72)	q = 1; p = 1;	-0.33 (-0.99) -0.4 (-1.24)
Bobbie Brooks	-1.7E-3 (-0.40)	0.769 (2.10)*	0.221 (0.50)	1.18 (1.61)*	-6.83E-4 (0.14)	0.0119* (2.14)*	q = 1;	0.28 (9.1)*
Empire Oil	-0.965 (-6.37)*	-0.136 (-0.17)	-1.355@ (-1.13)		0.964 (5.36)*	0.998* (5.55)*	q = 1; p = 1;	-0.16 (-1.10) -0.39 (-2.9)*
Inforex	-0.195 (0.00)	0.713 (0.35)	-2.647@ (-1.12)		-0.0201 (0.00)	0.0307 (0.00)	q = 1;	0.10 (2.7)*
Keydata	1.9E-3 (0.66)	0.418 (1.48)	-0.509 (-1.74)*	0.099 (0.33)	-2.7E-3 (-0.71)	-1.8E-4 (-0.05)		
Lawhorn	5.9E-3 (2.64)*	0.169 (0.65)	0.911 (2.34)*	0.159 (0.62)	-7.8E-3 (-2.46)*	-6.3E-3 (-1.63)*	p = 1;	-0.07 (-2.4)*
National Shoes	1.7E-3 (1.07)	3.6E-3 (0.03)	3.3E-3 (0.03)	-0.033@ (-0.185)	-2.2E-3 (-1.17)	1.7E-4 (0.09)	q = 1;	-0.06 (-2.4)*
Penn Dixie	6.2E-4 (0.1)	1.199 (3.08)*	0.547 (1.30)	-3.12 (-3.66)*	2.2E-3 (0.32)	-0.0022 (-0.31)	q = 1;	0.16 (4.9)*

Sam Solomon	-0.19 (-0.45)	0.43 (1.57)	1.7E-2@ (0.05)	-1.5E2@ (0.53)	0.189 (0.44)	0.193 (0.45)	q = 1; p = 1;	0.39 (1.52)	0.29 (1.08)
SBE	-1.843 (-0.01)	0.325 (0.95)	-0.063 (-0.18)	0.0696 (0.32)	6.2E-5 (0.19)	2.1E-3 (0.52)			
Unishelter	-1.0E-4 (0.00)	0.291 (0.51)	-0.516@ (-0.68)	-2.7E-3 (0.00)	2.5E-3 (0.00)		p = 1;	-0.01 (-0.30)	

Note: Parameters are explained in the text under equation 8; $F_1(B)$, $F_2(B)$ and $F_3(B)$ are polynomials in the backward shift operator, B. E_1, E_2 are estimates of abnormal stock return performance for periods 1 and 2.

@ Coefficient estimated after applying Dimson correction for infrequent trading. This correction is explained in the text.

* Significant T-statistic at the 0.05 level.

q,p: The q refers to the number of moving average parameters (i.e. coefficients of lagged errors in estimated stock returns) while p refers to the number of autoregressive parameters (i.e coefficient of lagged stock returns). The error processes considered here are the first-order mixed autoregressive moving average models with q and p = 1. The t-statistics indicate the significance of the corresponding error process parameter.

was adjusted for infrequent trading and autoregressive and moving average behavior of the stock return process.

SUMMARY

The results of the study did not resolve the issue of whether the market for the common stocks of Chapter 11 firms were priced efficiently in the sense of being able to analyze with a market model. The CAR analysis indicated that the "abnormal return" and the systematic risk of such common stocks increased after the firms filed for Chapter 11 protection. The results of the intervention analysis were, however, inconclusive, indicating that another form of risk measurement is needed when testing for abnormal performance. Reorganization risk may be this risk.

APPENDIX 1: INVESTMENT STYLES OF FUNDS THAT INVEST IN DISTRESSED FIRMS

The following is a summary of various investment styles of mutual funds that specialize in the investment of distressed companies. The description of the styles appeared in *Pensions & Investment Age,* March 6, 1989.[19]

- *Neuberger and Berman,* New York, plans to invest in troubled companies for individual and institutional investors. The company has been making bankruptcy investments for its own account for eight years. It will buy bank loans and other creditor positions with fund managers taking an active role in reorganizations.

- *Calhoun, Meehan & Co., Inc.,* Boston, has a fund that will be marketed to high-net-worth individuals. The "revitalization fund" buys companies with between $25 million and $250 million in sales and strong middle management teams with high variable margin and high fixed costs.

- *Oppenheimer & Co., Inc.,* New York, has invested its own capital in bankruptcies for more than ten years. It now offers the same opportunity to outside clients and foreign investors. Investments in distressed companies are diversified, generally in larger deals; no more than 3% to 4% is invested in the outstanding securities of any one company.

- *Trust Co. of the West,* Los Angeles, which invests along with its limited partners, likes to buy secured or senior debt instruments. It focuses on a few large, well-known companies, often that are still profitable, that it is confident will emerge from bankruptcy.

- *T. Rowe Price Associates,* Baltimore, an institutional investor, specializes in investment in debt securities and liabilities of companies experiencing significant financial difficulty.

- *The Foothill Group Inc.,* Los Angeles, invests its own and institutional contributions in companies in bankruptcy or in some stage of restructuring and prefers senior unsecured debt.

- *Paceholder Associates,* Cincinnati, has institutional clients invested in debt securities of a diversified portfolio of 25 to 30 troubled companies.

- *Morgens, Waterfall, Vintiadis & Co., Inc.,* New York, invests in distressed securities for individuals and foreign institutions. The firm claims to have a ten-year compound annualized return of 21.7%. The firm invests passively through a diversified portfolio with the aim of rebuilding rather than liquidating businesses.

• *Whitman Heffernan Rhein & Co., Inc.,* New York, has been in the bankruptcy business since 1974 when it was the investment bank M.J. Whitman & Co. Inc. It has been an independent firm since April 1987. Its limited partnership workout funds are open to pension funds for contributions and participation.

• *Magten Asset Management Corp.,* New York, buys stocks, bonds, and paid-in-kind preferred stock and has been in the bankruptcy business since 1978. The firm offers no limited partnership funds but has managed a partnership fund for a bank trust department. Many of its clients are tax-exempt institutions.

• *Recovery Equity Investors,* San Francisco, meant only for institutional investors, will invest in equity-oriented investments. It also plans to participate in management of bankrupt firms.

• *Halcyon Investments,* New York, meant for wealthy individual investors, invests mainly in public securities of bankrupt companies.

APPENDIX 2: THE ANATOMY OF A LEVERAGED BUYOUT

The following description of a typical LBO profile is taken from *The Anatomy of a Leveraged Buyout,* Salomon Brothers, January 1988.

An LBO is an acquisition of the stock or assets of an existing firm financed largely with long-term borrowings. Typically, the acquiring investor group would include the top management of the acquired firm, the deal-making investment bank, and the lending financial institutions—banks, insurance companies, pension funds, and so on. A majority of the LBOs possess the following elements:

• *Proven historical performance.* The LBO candidate must be capable of generating stable cash flow. Suitable candidates are therefore found, normally, in the noncyclical sector or have a demonstrated ability to weather business cycles.

• *Management.* Improvement on historical performance expected because of the involvement of the senior management team now vested with equity interests in the LBO.

• *Market leader.* Industry leadership positions for products of the LBO candidate in their markets. This will enable the firm to survive down cycles in the economy.

• *Mature products.* Such products do not require costly investment in research and development or other expenses for their upkeep and, as such, free up the cash flow for servicing the sizable debt that will be taken on by the LBO candidate.

• *Divisibility of assets.* The larger the break-up value, the more attractive the firm as an LBO candidate. The ready salability of assets could potentially supplement the much-needed cash flow in the initial years.

• *Minimal capital investment.* The LBO candidate would have to be parsimonious on capital needs to sustain its current and near-term level of operations.

• *Regulation, labor, hidden liabilities.* Extent of government regulation (could be a boon if regulation results in monopoly rights); existence of latent, contingent liabilities; and labor relations are other factors that need to be closely investigated before concluding the LBO.

A typical LBO process, from the date that the investor group decides to move forward to the close of the transaction, typically takes between four and six months to complete. Given below is a description of a likely schedule of steps that would be followed in an LBO:

Weeks 1–3   An investor group is formed, and a financial advisor is chosen. The inves-
                tor group forms a new corporation (NEWCO), which arranges the acqui-
                sition financing.

Weeks 4–7   The financial advisor proceeds with a valuation of the subject company,
                followed by the development of the transaction's structure. Using this
                information, the advisor, along with the investor group and if possible
                the subject company, drafts a confidential memorandum that outlines all
                the subject company's business. A list of potential lenders and additional
                investors is developed.

Weeks 8–10   Contact is made with potential lenders and investors. Those who express
                interest are sent the confidential memorandum and may also receive a
                presentation from the investor group. After two weeks, prospective
                investors/lenders are asked to make commitments, which in many cases,
                are subject to further due diligence.

Weeks 11–12   Potential investors/lenders conduct due diligence on the subject com-
                pany, including, if possible, the review of material that is too sensitive to
                include in the confidential memorandum and a tour of the subject's facil-
                ities.

Week 14   Formal written financing proposals are submitted by potential lenders/
                investors. The investor group selects an agent bank.

Weeks 14–15   Initial presentation of the proposal is made to the subject company's board
                of directors. In a transaction as complex as an LBO, lengthy and detailed
                negotiations are almost inevitable. Moreover, the transaction generally
                becomes public knowledge at this juncture, which may cause the subject
                company to be "in play," resulting in a "bidding war" among many
                investor groups. This was the case in the RJR Nabisco transaction.

Weeks 16–19   Assorted legal documents are drafted, including a merger agreement and
                a stock subscription agreement. These documents, together with the offer
                price, commitment letters from institutional investors/lenders, and a fair-
                ness opinion from an independent financial advisor, are presented to the
                board of directors for approval, followed by the execution of a merger
                agreement between the subject company and NEWCO. At this juncture,
                the LBO may be completed through either a one-step process involving
                a shareholder vote, or a two-step process involving a tender offer, fol-
                lowed by a shareholder vote.

The Final Step It is more common for the transaction to be completed through a two-
                step process. As was the case in the $3.6 billion LBO of Fort Howard
                Corporation (1988), the NEWCO (in this case, FH Acquisition) com-
                menced a tender offer for all of the outstanding common stock on July 1,
                1988. Upon the expiration of the offer on August 8, 1988, FH Acquisition
                purchased the tendered shares. Subsequently, FH Acquisition filed a proxy
                statement with the SEC seeking clearance for the transaction. After re-
                ceiving SEC approval, FH Acquisition mailed the proxy to shareholders
                and, on October 24, 1988, convened a shareholders' meeting to approve
                the merger agreement. On October 25, 1988, the surviving company, Fort
                Howard Corporation, completed its public high-yield financing. The time
                involved from the commencement of the tender offer to the completion
                of the financing was 125 days.

In all cases the new company will exhibit a highly leveraged capital structure in
which the total capital generally exceeds 85%. Given below are approximate

range of the various elements of a company's capitalization subsequent to an LBO.

<table>
<tr><td colspan="2" align="center">**Approximate percentage
of capitalization**</td></tr>
<tr><td>Senior Debt</td><td>40–70</td></tr>
<tr><td>Subordinated Debt</td><td>10–30</td></tr>
<tr><td>Preferred Stock</td><td>5–10</td></tr>
<tr><td>Common Stock</td><td>5–15</td></tr>
</table>

NOTES

1. Bankruptcy filings in 1987 were triple the number filed in 1980. *The Wall Street Journal,* July 14, 1988, p. 29.

2. Altman (1981) describes the lack of liquidity as technical insolvency, or insolvency in the equity sense. Bankruptcy insolvency occurs when a firm's total liabilities are greater than its total assets.

3. See *The Wall Street Journal,* January 21, 1988, p. 1.

4. See *The Wall Street Journal,* January 21, 1988, p. 1.

5. Options are rights to buy or sell the underlying instrument (e.g., a stock) at an agreed upon price on or before the expiration date. While the maximum loss that could be incurred in buying an option is the option premium (the purchase price), maximum gain is open-ended.

6. *Forbes,* October 6, 1988, p. 147.

7. See *The Wall Street Journal,* July 6, 1988, p. 4.

8. Arbel, Carvell, and Strebel (1983) found that the stocks of firms neglected by analysts earn excess risk-adjusted returns or abnormal returns.

9. Dewing (1931) attributed most bankruptcies to some form of management incompetence. Argenti (1976) summarized some management deficiencies as those resulting from fraud, ignoring technology changes, reluctance to tighten cost control standards, ignoring cash flows when making investment decisions, and expanding the firm too quickly by floating excessive amounts of debt.

10. *Pension & Investment Age,* June 27, 1988, p. 4.

11. *The Wall Street Journal,* December 29, 1988, p. C1.

12. This section is based on Moeller (1986).

13. See the *New York Times,* November 17, 1988, p. D1.

14. See *The Wall Street Journal,* April 14, 1989, p. C1.

15. *The Wall Street Journal,* April 14, 1989, p. C5.

16. See *The Wall Street Journal,* November 15, 1988, p. C1.

17. Most of this information was obtained from current business periodicals dated around the time of the filings of these firms. Information was taken from *Financial World,* November 15, 1982; *Forbes,* March 15, 1982; and *Dun's Business Month,* September 1982.

18. Expected return $E(R_{jt})$ in a market model is estimated as $E(R_{jt}) = a_j + b_j R_{mt}$ where the returns on security j is simply assumed to be linearly related to the return on the "market" portfolio, R_{mt}.

19. Reprinted here with permission from Crain Communications.

The Environment and Bankrupt Firms

Managers, lenders, and investors alike ask: Why do companies fail? Bank lending officers spend hours poring over financial statements to predict whether a company is a good risk, whether it will survive long enough to pay back the loan with interest. Investors study the same financial statements, trying to determine if a firm is a good investment risk. Will the firm not merely survive but grow to yield a respectable return on their investment? Managers may want to identify the factors that cause firms to fail in the first place and what is likely to happen in the wake of failure. This chapter discusses the reasons for firm failure, the events that occur when a firm enters financial distress, the effect of reorganization, and why investors who invest in failed firms *may* be able to earn very high excess returns.

REASONS FOR FAILURE

Not all failures necessarily result in the collapse and dissolution of a firm.[1] Economic failure usually signifies that a company can not earn enough in revenues to cover its costs. It can also mean that the rate of earnings on its investments does not cover its opportunity cost of funds. Some even consider a shortfall of actual returns below expected returns a sign of economic failure. Investors, in other words, can invest their money in other companies and earn a higher return while incurring the level of risk comparable to an investment in the failing firm.

Although financial failure is a less-ambiguous term than economic failure, it has two commonly understood definitions. A firm can be considered a failure if it can not meet its current obligations as they fall due, even though its total assets may exceed its total liabilities. This is defined as technical insolvency. A firm is a failure, or bankrupt, if its total liabilities exceed a fair valuation of its total assets—that is to say, the real net worth of the company is negative. A comprehensive and practically useful notion of *business failure* refers to the inability of the firm to meet its financial obligations.

We are mainly interested in firms that have failed in the sense that they have been forced to file for Chapter 11 court protection. These firms may be technically insolvent or truly bankrupt. The term "bankrupt" will be used to identify firms that have failed and have filed for Chapter 11, while firms that have failed but not filed will be called "firms in financial distress."

Companies fail either because of economic conditions beyond the control of management or because of conditions that exist inside a firm. Some economists and managers would sharpen this broad and simple statement and say instead that it is not external factors themselves that result in firms going bankrupt, it is the lack of ability and willingness of managers to cope with a changing environment. Over the years, many studies have been done of the factors that cause firms to be unable to meet their obligations. There is a general consensus that, by far, the major source of business failure is management incompetence. Broadly defined, management incompetence includes a lack of experience in that particular line of business; familiarity with the product market but unbalanced experience in one or more of the management functions, such as sales, finance, production, research, or planning; lack of prescience to anticipate unfavorable industry developments; or sheer hubris leading to underestimation of competition. Management incompetence thus accounts for almost 90 percent of all business failures with the remainder due to natural causes (earthquakes, floods, fires, wars, and other "acts of God") and criminal frauds (usually, spectacular cases).

Possible management deficiencies cited in the academic literature can make quite an extensive list (Dewing, 1931; Argenti, 1976):

1. Ignoring product technology changes
2. Fraud
3. Maintaining a poor intercompany communication system
4. Reluctance to establish tight cost control standards
5. Ignoring cash flow when making investment decisions
6. Expanding the firm too quickly by floating excessive amounts of debt
7. Increasing sales at the expense of profits
8. Concentrating too many resources into one large project

ILLUSTRATIVE RECENT BANKRUPTCIES

Since 1980, more firms have failed than failed in the 50 years after the stock market crash in 1929.[2] High interest rates, a long persistent recession, and climbing debt ratios may have been the principal culprits during the early part of the 1980s. Other factors contributing to a high rate of bankruptcy are expensive labor costs, additional government regulation, increased competition from overseas, and changing technology.

The effect of expensive labor union contracts has forced a number of firms into bankruptcy. An example is Wilson Foods, which filed for Chapter 11 relief in April 1983. The company claimed that its future cash flow was in jeopardy because competitors had obtained wage concessions from the United Food and Commercial Workers International Union to which Wilson's union workers were not subject. Another example is Continental Airlines, which also cited high labor costs as the reason it was forced to file for bankruptcy. Continental was hoping to blunt the competitive advantage of nonunion carriers that had developed after airline deregulation.

Investors may ask whether these reasons for filing will protect companies from creditors. Are the arguments legally justifiable? Is it legitimate to claim that a company with higher labor costs is entitled to relief under bankruptcy reorganization? It is easy to see why labor officials believed that the bankruptcy law was being used to "bust" unions.

On February 22, 1984, the U.S. Supreme Court resolved conflicting lower court decisions on the issue when it ruled that union contracts can be voided unilaterally if the long-term solvency of a firm is at stake and if a bankruptcy court judge agrees to the cancellation. At the same time the Court rejected the union requests that Chapter 11 companies should be required to negotiate contract changes while they are under court protection. Continental Airlines' position against its unions was also upheld by a Houston bankruptcy court.

Fighting expensive labor contracts with the 1978 Bankruptcy Code does have its risks. On the one hand, a company filing hopes it will be allowed to start over without the use of unionized labor. Instead of getting a reborn enterprise, however, stockholders could wind up with no company at all, for all companies filing under Chapter 11 are vulnerable to liquidation.

In the case of Continental Airlines, management strategy has paid off as of 1988. A company spokesperson stated at the time of the airline's filing that if the firm had not filed it would have gone broke, although critics noted that Continental had about $50 million in cash at that time. Even that amount, however, was not enough to cover the airline's payroll. While under Chapter 11, Continental downsized its operation. Some 9,000 employees were terminated, and service was reduced by a full

75%. Since that time, of course, Continental has increased its payroll and expanded its service. The airline claims that the ultimate reason the company filed for bankruptcy was that management believed Continental was worth more to its shareholders as a going concern than as a liquidated one.

Not keeping pace with technology changes is another reason companies often go bankrupt. Shareholders may really become losers in this case, as managers fail to respond to research and development advances made by other firms. Bowmar Instrument was successful in the calculator business before Texas Instruments and Hewlett Packard entered the market, drove down calculator prices, and forced Bowmar into Chapter 11. Bowmar lost market share rapidly when the other companies competed based on price. For lack of investment in research and development for future calculator projects, Bowmar had nothing new to offer and soon became overstocked with inventories. Over the last few years many high-technology firms have faced a similar plight.

A corollary example is Computer Devices, a David that tried to compete with a Goliath—IBM—which won in the end. Computer Devices had an excellent personal computer that, according to many in the business, was better than the IBM personal computers available at the time. The company's management, however, decided not to make the product IBM-compatible. Despite a state-of-the-art personal computer, Computer Devices was a single-product company, undercapitalized, and with a non-IBM-compatible offering to boot. The firm eventually filed for Chapter 11 in the face of declining sales and nonexistent credit lines.

Two of the biggest bankruptcies in the history of the United States (not counting the most recent megabankruptcy of Texaco) are attributable to management incompetence or arrogance. W.T. Grant, a gigantic retailer that eventually was forced to liquidate, and Wickes, a building supply firm that underwent reorganization, are classic examples of mismanagement of current assets and short-term debt in the face of expansion. Investors in these firms who bought the stock after the filing occurred, however, would not have been hurt.

W.T. Grant had a relaxed accounts receivable credit policy; the company took on high-risk clients. The easy credit policy resulted in substantial cash drain for the firm, as bad debts were enormous. Poor inventory management in addition frequently meant that Grant's retail stores had little to sell.

Wickes had a negative net worth of $2 billion when it filed for bankruptcy on April 4, 1982. Management had relied on short-term debt to finance operations in a period of rising interest rates. The firm had overexpanded through acquisitions and had not issued long-term debt or equity to finance these purchases. The banks finally cut off Wickes's credit, and the firm was forced to file for Chapter 11. In this case, bankruptcy was healthy for its victim. The company reorganized successfully, emerging in better shape than before. Unproductive assets were sold off and liabilities restructured.

Penn Central is another example of a firm that benefited from reorganization. After ridding itself of the railroad and $4 billion in claims, it emerged as a conglomerate in energy and real estate with $1 billion in assets. Penn Central has been profitable ever since.

In 1982 the once-profitable Manville Corporation blazed a legal trail when it filed for bankruptcy protection to defend itself from the thousands of lawsuits brought by victims of the asbestos produced by the company. In August 1985, A.H. Robins sought protection under Chapter 11 of the federal Bankruptcy Code to freeze thousands of lawsuits by women hurt by the Dalkon Shield intrauterine device produced by the company. These are two spectacular cases of financial distress caused by either inadequate product testing or lack of management appreciation of the magnitude of liability inherent in their products. Both the firms have since emerged from bankruptcy as reorganized firms after having set aside sizable trust funds for the benefit of the claimants. A.H. Robins was acquired by American Home Products, which created a $2.38 billion trust fund for the Dalkon Shield claimants.

The largest bankruptcy filing in U.S. history was made on April 12, 1987, when Texaco filed for court protection from creditors in order to forestall enforcement of a $10.3 billion judgment against it awarded to Pennzoil by a Texas jury in December 1985. That judgment arose from Pennzoil's claim that Texaco's 1984 acquisition of Getty Oil Company had illegally interfered with a prior Pennzoil contract to acquire part of Getty. Texaco's four-year-old legal donnybrook with Pennzoil ended on April 7, 1988, when it emerged from the legal proceedings after its plan of reorganization was approved by the court. As part of the reorganization, Texaco ended up paying Pennzoil $3 billion as full and final settlement of their $11 billion dispute. Much has been written about Texaco management's initial complacency in meeting Pennzoil's challenge of its acquisition of Getty Oil. Part of Texaco's lack of vigilance could also be attributed to the generally permissive environment of the 1980s that tolerated mergers and acquisitions of increasingly larger amounts. Whether it was management hubris, incompetence, or a cavalier attitude toward legal contracts, the fact remains that this was the most unusual reason for financial failure.

ENTERING FINANCIAL DISTRESS

Although many factors come into play as causes of firm failure, what should be of interest to potential investors in Chapter 11 firms is the macroeconomic environment confronting a firm entering reorganization.

No matter what the cause of a firm's difficulties, certain responses can be expected from the management of a firm in financial distress.

The first sign that a firm may be in trouble financially usually is that it cannot pay its creditors. There have been special cases in recent years where firms have filed for Chapter 11 not because they could not pay current bills but because they could not pay future ones. When Continental Airlines filed for Chapter 11 in 1984, it was not because of poor current cash flow but because a new labor contract made it impossible, or so management claimed, to earn future cash flow.

A similar case is represented by the Manville Corporation, which filed for Chapter 11 in 1982. The company was on the losing end of a decision that would cost it billions of dollars. People harmed by the asbestos the company made brought a class-action suit. When the jury found in favor of the plaintiffs, the company booked on its balance sheet a liability to cover the amount of the settlement awarded. With such a large liability, the company was no longer solvent—its liabilities and shareholders' equity were less than its total assets. The firm believed it had no choice but to file for court protection from its creditors under Chapter 11.

Under normal circumstances, however, firms enter financial distress because they do not have the cash flow to pay their creditors. As creditors begin to pressure delinquent firms, management can react in a variety of ways. The company may violate debt covenants by defaulting on interest payments. Shareholder dividends may be omitted, although this usually does not happen until the firm has absorbed months of negative cash flow. Management may attempt to reduce costs by obtaining concessions from its labor force and suppliers. Failing in that approach, it may begin to close plants, lay off salaried workers, sell off unprofitable divisions, or take other actions in an attempt to reduce overhead costs. Figure 3.1 schematically represents this macro view of events.

A key to survival for a Chapter 11 firm tends to be a firm's ability to reorganize its capital structure and start over. Management may begin to look for new financial support from its bankers and other general creditors. A shift in policy may be made, as management seeks new ways to increase cash flow. Different types of projects or lines of business may be taken on under such circumstances. The capital markets respond to these management actions by reevaluating the risk and return relationship of securities of firms in financial distress. In most cases, trading in these firms shifts from the major exchanges to regional exchanges and the over-the-counter market. Institutional investors usually lead the way in selling off these securities as they become more speculative. Credit markets demand higher interest rates on new loans if any financing is available at all. Other factors affecting financially distressed firms are bankruptcy costs and increased risk of a firm's expected cash flows. Although bankruptcy costs have been demonstrated empirically,

Figure 3.1
Macro View of Events Affecting Chapter 11 Firms

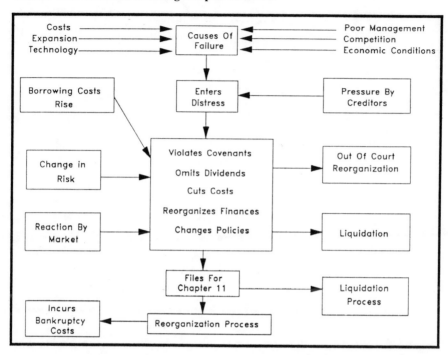

there is ongoing academic debate (see Haugen and Senbet, 1978 and Warner, 1977b) on whether they are high or low and on how the risk of future cash flows really changes.[3] Possible management response to financial distress by way of reorganization is shown schematically in Figure 3.2.

Despite the factors discussed above, filing for bankruptcy may not be the best way for small firms to address their business problems when creditors come knocking. In 1987, 17,142 companies filed for bankruptcy under Chapter 11. Of those firms, by July 1988, 6,722 were still in business under the same ownership. But this masks a crucial distinction. While fully 69% of large firms (revenues above $100 million) that filed for bankruptcy in 1987 were by July 1988 still in business, for the small firm (revenues less than $25 million), only 30% were still in business under the same ownership.[4]

EFFECT OF REORGANIZATION ON A FIRM

Understanding the internal environment faced by a Chapter 11 firm is as important for potential investors as recognizing the macro dimension.

Figure 3.2
Reorganization

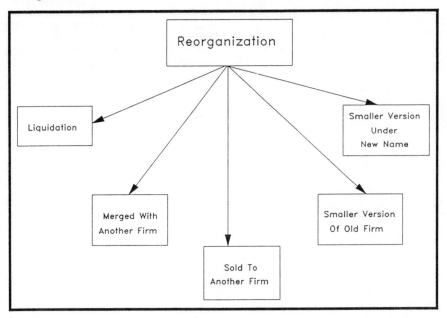

Figure 3.3 illustrates the usual reactions of investors to the plight of a Chapter 11 firm.

As the company experiences financial distress, the market reacts by readjusting its expectations on the risk and return relationship of a bankrupt company's securities (see Altman, 1969a; Westerfield, 1970; Aharony et al., 1980; and Clark and Weinstein, 1983, for a summary of bankruptcy event studies). The total variance of a bankrupt firm's returns increases drastically as the firm approaches formal bankruptcy. It is logical to ask whether this increase in risk is rewarded with extra high returns. In fact, there are four reasons why it is possible for an investor to earn a high profit from buying the stocks of companies that have filed for Chapter 11: (1) missing information, (2) court valuation of assets, (3) wealth transfer from bondholders to shareholders, and (4) appeal of management.

Missing Information

One of the reasons for the mispricing (incorrect pricing) of Chapter 11 stocks is the lack of information about these firms. Typically, fewer buyers than sellers are interested in bankrupt firm securities. Institutional investors sell them because the funds they manage often have restric-

Figure 3.3
Micro-Environment of Chapter 11 Firms

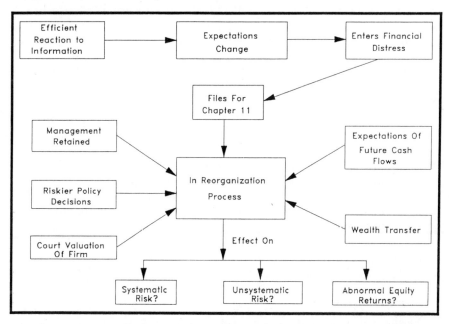

tions barring them from holding such securities. Stocks of Chapter 11 firms also trade infrequently, sometimes offered only by dealers. Investors interested in ferreting out such opportunities will not get much help from professional analysts. The large brokerage firms consider bankrupt companies so risky and complex that they shy away from publishing reports on them. Several firms, such as Drexel Burnham Lambert, Merrill Lynch, and Bear, Stearns, do make markets in the securities of bankrupt companies. They report that their clients—apart from other traders—generally do their own research.

Court Valuation of Assets

According to some experts (Weston, 1977), we might look at a bankrupt firm as a new organization that must readjust to its new circumstances. New management, capital, and objectives will alter its identity. Expected future earnings will not be known for some time. For this reason, valuation of bankrupt firms is difficult and subject to a large degree of uncertainty.

Courts usually have followed SEC guidelines, not market reaction, when determining a firm's reorganization value. Traditionally they have overestimated the value of the reorganized firm in order to give something to junior creditors and stockholders. There are a number of reasons why the legal system has been structured to protect the shareholders of bankrupt firms (see Meckling, 1977; Schuchman, 1977):

1. Before the adoption of the original Chapter X and XI bankruptcy codes, it was believed that junior creditors and small groups of unorganized investors could be treated inequitably by other creditors who were in a position to take advantage of a forced liquidation.

2. It has been argued that business investment would decline if shareholders were not granted any rights in the event of firm failure. Because future growth of general equity investment would be inhibited, all businesses would suffer as a result.

3. The marketplace cannot be used to determine a value for a failed firm because the courts believe that such an estimate reflects only a specific time. The courts have stated that they believe the SEC does a better job at incorporating future expected earnings estimates into the valuation equation than does the marketplace.

4. The courts claim that senior secured creditors possess the real power in reorganizations. If they do not assert their rights, this does not prove shareholders have too much power or that they abuse what power they retain. Thus, the courts dismiss the concept that the bankruptcy law itself allows a wealth transfer to occur.

5. Finally, the courts claim no empirical evidence exists to determine whether wealth transfer to shareholders occurs, or if shareholders end up with more wealth than they should from a bankruptcy proceeding. However, the shares of a firm in bankruptcy are almost always diluted during restructuring, because bondholders usually are paid off with a package of new bonds and some stock and cash. Thus, shareholders who as a group own 100 percent of a company going into bankruptcy may emerge with only 20 percent of the total equity. This process is known as a reverse stock split. When Sambos reorganized, for example, current stockholders had to turn over 125 shares of the old company for each share of the new company.

Wealth Transfer from Bondholders to Shareholders

In general, shareholders can be viewed as holding a call option on a levered firm (a firm with debt).[5] The value of their option would increase with an increase in the riskiness of the firm's cash flow. Thus, having taken on a certain level of debt, there exists an incentive for shareholders to increase the riskiness of the projects undertaken by the firm. This change would result in a wealth transfer from bondholders to shareholders.

Bondholders commit their funds to projects with certain expected risk and return characteristics. If the company uses monies obtained from the bond issue to finance riskier projects than the bondholders expected, shareholders not bondholders would be the recipients of any excess returns reaped from the riskier project. If the riskier project fails, though, the value of the firm will decline, and stockholders will not exercise their "option." Rather, they will let the firm become bankrupt and the remaining assets fall to creditors. The equityholders' maximum loss, in this case, will be limited to the initial price they paid to acquire the stock.

Creditors do attempt to control such circumstances by placing covenants on debt issues and monitoring management's practices. If a firm in financial distress can seek court protection from its creditors, however, the value of the shareholders' call option is restored and not subject to any creditor restrictions. One expert (Miller, 1977) puts it this way:

Gambling with other people's money would indeed be an artistic way of making a living, if only one could find the other people to supply the bankroll at the riskless rate of interest. In general one can't. But if a corporation is close to default, and if it can get court protection from foreclosure, it may have a close equivalent.

What does this all mean for investors interested in buying the stock of bankrupt firms? If management begins making aggressive, and somewhat riskier, policy decisions after a firm files for Chapter 11, any excess profits that the firm earns will go to shareholders and not to bondholders. All bondholders have done is lend their money to a firm at a fixed rate for a fixed amount of risk. If management uses this money while under the protection of the court to invest in speculative projects—and wins—the shareholders are the beneficiaries.

One study on the railroad industry demonstrated that although the value of equity fell to one-third of its original amount after bankruptcy, the value of senior secured debt fell even more drastically. Financial distress affected common stock returns first, and then debt returns. After bankruptcy, however, the common stock price rose before that of any other class of security. While technically the market value of a bankrupt firm's equity should be zero when the firm's market value falls below the par value of its senior debt securities, this was not the case with bankrupt railroads. Prebankruptcy owners did lose absolute wealth, but their stock was not worthless. In fact, the equity value of bankrupt railroads increased as a percentage of total firm value (Gordon, 1971).

There is other evidence that wealth may be transferred to the shareholders of bankrupt firms from the creditors. A 1977 seminar (Moore, 1977) on the economics of bankruptcy reform addressing the wealth transfer question reached several conclusions:

1. Some practices in corporate bankruptcy proceedings inherently seem to favor debtors over creditors. Shareholders and managers of firms in Chapter 11 may have an advantage over creditors because of the management power they retain.

2. The incentive to make riskier policy decisions during a Chapter 11 proceeding may cause a transfer of wealth from creditors to debtor shareholders.

3. The valuation practices of the SEC in bankruptcy proceedings tend to work against the absolute-priority rule that is intended to favor creditors.

A more recent development is the creation of "equity committees" to protect the rights of shareholders. These equity committees have become vocal in determining the outcome of bankruptcy proceedings. In the megacontests, like those of Texaco and A.H. Robins, shareholders exerted great influence and weakened the dominant grip of management and creditor groups.

In Texaco's bankruptcy case, a committee representing shareholders galvanized a $3 billion compromise settlement of the company's $10.3 billion fight with Pennzoil. The committee also successfully pushed Texaco management to weaken antitakeover defenses, contending that those measures entrenched the interests of the oil giant's top officers. In the A.H. Robins case, the equity committee challenged management's efforts to merge with a French drug maker, Sanofi S.A. The group prodded significantly higher bids from two other suitors, Rorer Group and American Home Products, the eventual winner. By holding separate, private bargaining sessions with all three bidders, the committee helped turn the Robins proceedings into an auction and ultimately saw its favorite prevail.[6]

Appeal of Management

Even if bankruptcy proceedings do not serve to oust poor management, there are several circumstances that may allow Chapter 11 stocks to earn excess returns. First, the personal appeal of a firm's chief operating officer could be essential for the support of the financial markets for a firm's reorganization plan (Dewing, 1931). Second, creditors may have reason to support the retention of the current management and its reorganization plan. Their support may prevent the conversion of assets to cash dividends by a management expecting to be ousted in the event of filing (Meckling, 1977).

Retaining management should not in and of itself be an indication that a Chapter 11 firm can earn excess returns. The effect of retaining management, though, has certain consequences. For one, retaining management allows a quick, relatively inexpensive reorganization plan to be accepted by all parties, and the firm has a chance to emerge from Chapter 11 financially strong. Existing management will have another chance to run a successful operation.

SUMMARY

Business failure refers to the inability of a firm to meet its financial obligations. These firms have failed in the sense that they have been forced to file for Chapter 11 court protection. Technical insolvency occurs when the firm fails to meet its current obligations owing to inadequate cash flows. This can occur even when the firm's total assets exceed its total liabilities. A firm is bankrupt when its total liabilities exceed the market value of its total assets. Such a firm will have a negative net worth. A bankrupt firm generally will be forced to file for protection under Chapter 11; the technically insolvent firm, though financially distressed, by negotiating with its creditors for temporary reprieve, may be able to avoid filing for bankruptcy altogether.

Companies fail essentially because of management incompetence. Even when external factors relating to the economy are cited as the reason for the failure, it is the management's failure to respond to changing economic conditions that is to blame. A broad definition of management incompetence would include lack of relevant product line or market experience; lack of one or more functional experience in sales, finance, production, research, or planning; an inability to foresee emerging unfavorable industry developments; or arrogance leading to underestimation of competition. Investors identifying the fundamental factors affecting a bankrupt firm will follow a process similar to the one they should use for a nonbankrupt firm. First, they will want an assessment of whether a firm in Chapter 11 will liquidate or reorganize. If the company liquidates, secured debt issues are always preferable to nonsecured issues. In the Braniff case, for example, the airline announced that its unsecured debtors could receive only ten cents on the dollar if the firm were liquidated rather than reorganized.

Investors may have to evaluate the type of bankrupt security—stocks or bonds—to invest in. While the courts have held that senior secured creditors possess the real power in reorganizations, there are instances of wealth transfer from bondholders to shareholders owing to built-in incentives for management to adopt aggressive and risky policies while under court protection. Investors should also evaluate the various times they may choose to take a position in a bankrupt stock. Immediately after filing offers the most risk, as the balance of the assets and liabilities remains uncertain. At the same time, however, the stock is at its lowest. A month or two after filing, when court-appointed accountants evaluate the bankrupt firm's financial statements, the data becomes more reliable.

Saxon Industries, for example, filed in mid-April 1982, yet it was not until June 1982 that the company disclosed its inventories had been overstated by at least $24 million. This circumstance would have been costly for an investor who jumped into the firm's stock or bonds immediately after the bankruptcy filing.

The other time an investor could choose to purchase the equity of a bankrupt firm is after the announcement of the reorganization plan. This strategy may avoid the unpleasant surprise of a reverse split announcement, such as in the Itel case. Itel's bonds traded at $250 before its reorganization plan was announced and at $480 right after. Investment risk (ex-post) in this instance was similar to that of holding Treasury bills.

NOTES

1. The definitions of failure are based on Chapter 31 of Weston and Copeland (1986).

2. In 1987, 17,142 companies filed for Chapter 11—nearly triple the 6,298 companies that filed in 1980, says the Administrative Office of the U.S. Courts. *The Wall Street Journal,* July 14, 1988, p. 29.

3. In the massive case of A.H. Robins, for example, U.S. District Judge Robert Merhige, Jr. told lawyers that their fees "border on being utterly ridiculous." In November 1987 he took the unusual step of ordering an end to all attorney payments until the conclusion of the case. Before the judge halted the payments, the lawyers had collected about $12.2 million for work done since the company sought court protection in August 1985. *The Wall Street Journal,* February 23, 1988, p. 33.

4. For a company with annual sales of about $5 million, fees for lawyers, accountants, consultants, and other court costs range from $50,000 to $250,000. Small companies cannot withstand that kind of financial buffeting. See *The Wall Street Journal,* July 14, 1988, p. 29.

5. A call option gives the holder the right to *buy* the underlying asset (stock) at a predetermined price (exercise price) on or before the expiration date.

6. See *The Wall Street Journal,* January 21, 1988, p.1.

The Law and Reorganization of Bankrupt Firms

Historically, the topic of bankruptcy and its economic ramifications on a firm's value has been studied within the context of determining bankruptcy costs and their impact on a firm's risk and return.These studies were basically concerned with explaining the *ex ante* effect of bankruptcy on the value of a firm. Beginning with the early 1970s and the bankruptcy of the Penn Central Railroad, some economists expressed concern about the impact of corporate failures on our economic system. Analyses were undertaken in an attempt to understand how U.S. bankruptcy laws affected the redistribution of investor wealth. From these studies the consensus came that the laws needed revision since they tended to delay the recovery of financially distressed firms and often resulted in the inefficient use and reallocation of resources. On July 14, 1978, the National Bankruptcy Act was amended to become the Bankruptcy Reform Act of 1978. This new code treats the common equityholders of distressed firms more leniently than the old law and makes it easier for these firms to file for reorganization.

When a business firm is unable to meet its obligations, the outcome is any one of three possibilities: the firm continues in its original form, merges or is acquired by another firm, or it ceases to exist as a firm. It will be useful to have an overview of the alternative methods of dealing with business failure. A framework for this overview is provided in Figure 4.1.

These outcomes can be achieved either through relatively informal, out-of-court or formal, legal, court-supervised procedures. The most in-

Investing in Financially Distressed Firms

Figure 4.1
Consequences of Business Failure

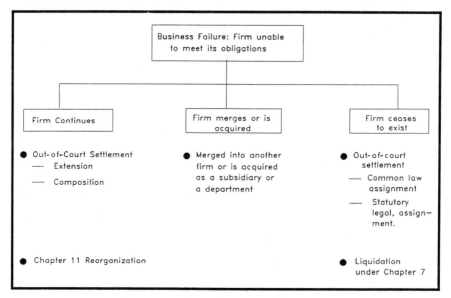

formal out-of-court procedure is to postpone the date when payment is required or give an extension. If the creditors agree to take some fraction of what is owed as full settlement, this is called a composition. If a firm has to be liquidated, a relatively informal procedure exists called the common law assignment. The assets of a firm are assigned to a trustee who liquidates the assets and distributes the proceeds on a pro rata basis to the creditors.

The formal, legal proceedings could lead the failing firm to be reorganized, merged into another firm, or be liquidated. The Bankruptcy Reform Act of 1978 provided for a Chapter 11 reorganization. This represents a formal court-supervised procedure for scaling down or modifying the claims of creditors, a form of composition. In a merger, the firm's identity may be continued as a separate subsidiary or its identity may be lost through absorption into other operations. Finally a firm may cease to exist through an assignment or by liquidation under Chapter 7 of the bankruptcy act. Under Chapter 7 proceedings, there is much more court supervision involved in the processes for liquidating the assets of the firm that has failed.

This chapter covers the voluntary and legal, court-supervised methods of restructuring a firm; it also provides a description of the original Chapter X and XI bankruptcy laws and illustrates how the new Chapter 11 bankruptcy law is different from the old and better for stockholders.

EXTENSION AND COMPOSITION

Extension and composition represent voluntary concessions by creditors.[1] Companies that are in financial distress but do not wish to file for Chapter 11 relief are most likely to try to get creditors to extend the due date of required payments (extension); they may also seek creditors to reduce their claims voluntarily (composition). Both methods are intended to keep the distressed firm in business and to avoid court costs of a legal remedy. Creditors are often willing to accommodate a firm by absorbing a temporary loss in the hopes that the company will emerge from its problems with a stable financial position. This could provide long-run benefits for a creditor.

Procedurally, a meeting of the company and its creditors is held. At the meeting, the creditors appoint a committee consisting of the largest creditors as a majority. The committee is assigned the task of investigating the financial position of the distressed firm and of preparing a formal plan for an extension or composition of claims. Three conditions are usually necessary to make an extension or a composition feasible:

1. The debtor must be a good moral risk, in the sense of seeking to honor obligations and not diverting the business's assets to personal use and advantage.
2. The debtor must show ability to make a recovery.
3. General business conditions must be favorable to recovery.

An extension is usually preferred by creditors as it provides payment in full. In a composition, a pro rata cash settlement is made. The creditors must believe that the company can solve its problems, but they also want to exercise control over the company's credit decisions until they have been paid. Sometimes the creditor committee insists that some assets be sold and the cash be held in escrow in case the company defaults again. Stockholders may also be asked to submit their shares to escrow until the company's debts become current. In a composition, the creditors take a percentage of the debt owed them in cash. The percentage could be as low as 10%. If the company's financial situation is dire, creditors may be asked not only to take 10 cents on a dollar of their claims, but also to extend the time the company has to repay the debt.

OUT-OF-COURT, VOLUNTARY SETTLEMENTS

The advantages of voluntary settlements are that they are informal and quick, in that a company can start on the road to financial solvency sooner than with a court-imposed settlement. The procedure is the most economical and results in the largest return to creditors.

A major disadvantage for creditors of not insisting that a company file for Chapter 11 is that management is left in unsupervised control of the firm. Erosion of assets could occur in that the management could try to bleed the company of cash without paying the creditors. A second disadvantage is that small creditors may refuse to take less than what is due them resulting in a delayed or impossible settlement.

COURT-DIRECTED INVOLUNTARY SETTLEMENTS

Reorganization is a form of extension or composition of the firm's obligations. Regardless of the legal procedure followed, reorganization processes have several features in common:

1. The firm is insolvent either because it is unable to meet cash obligations as they come due or because claims on the firm exceed its assets.
2. New funds must be raised for working capital and for property rehabilitation.
3. The operating and managerial causes of difficulty must be discovered and eliminated.

The reorganization plan must be fair to all parties and must be feasible. The company must emerge from reorganization as a going concern. When a company enters financial distress a decision must be made whether the company should be liquidated or rehabilitated. This decision is based upon the value of the firm as a going concern versus the liquidated value of its assets.

Standard of Fairness

The basic doctrine of fairness states that claims must be recognized in the order of their legal and contractual priority. Junior claimants, such as common stockholders, can participate only to the extent that they make an additional cash contribution to the reorganization of the firm. The steps of determining fairness are as follows:

1. An estimate of future sales must be made.
2. An analysis of operating conditions must be made so that the future earnings on sales can be estimated.
3. A determination must be made of the capitalization rate to be applied to the estimated future earnings to obtain an indicated value of the company's properties.
4. A determination of the amounts to be distributed to the claimants must be made.

Standards of Feasibility

The primary test of feasibility is that the fixed charges on the income of the corporation after reorganization are amply covered by earnings. Actions may be needed to improve the earning power of the company.

1. The maturities of debt obligations are often extended, and some unsecured debt is converted into common stock.
2. New management may be needed.
3. Plant and equipment modernization must occur before the company can operate efficiently and compete on a cost basis.
4. Obsolete inventories must be disposed of.
5. Divisions may have to be sold to other companies. Sometimes companies need to develop a new goal or mission since old ones may be outdated technologically. Many firms get into financial difficulties because they expand too rapidly and do not have the management expertise or capital to sustain a competitive edge or growth in a particular industry.

The Priority of Claims

Chapter 5 of the new bankruptcy law sets out the priority of expenses and claims that must occur during a reorganization:

1. Secured creditors receive the proceeds from the sales of property pledged. If the value of the property is less than the amount of the loan the difference between the value and the loan becomes an unsecured claim. Secured creditors are not forced to accept only the depressed value of the property.
2. Trustees' costs involved in the proceedings.
3. Expenses after an involuntary case has begun but before a trustee is appointed.
4. Wages due workers if earned within three months prior to filing; the amount can not exceed $2,000 per person.
5. Claims for unpaid contributions to employee benefit plans to have been paid within six months prior to the filing.
6. Unsecured claims for customer deposits, with a maximum of $900 per individual.
7. Taxes due to federal, state, county, and any other governmental agencies.
8. Unfunded pension plan liabilities have a priority over general creditors up to 30% of the sum of common and preferred equity.
9. General or unsecured creditors including trade creditors, unsecured loans, and debenture bondholders, and the unsatisfied portions of the secured loans and unfunded pension plan liabilities.
10. Subordinated debtholders.

11. Preferred stockholders.

12. Common stockholders receive anything that remains.

The absolute priority doctrine calls for exactly following the above ordering. The relative priority doctrine is less rigid in view of the uncertainties of estimating the current value of future streams of cash flow. It seeks to preserve some stake in the company for junior claimants. Under Chapter 11 of the new law most reorganization plans follow the relative priority doctrine while liquidations distribute cash according to the absolute priority doctrine.

LIQUIDATION: ASSIGNMENT VERSUS BANKRUPTCY

There are two ways a company can be liquidated. Common law assignment is a liquidation procedure that does not go through the courts, while bankruptcy is a legal procedure carried out under the jurisdiction of special courts in which a firm is formally liquidated and creditors' claims are completely discharged.

Under a common law assignment the company transfers title to all of its assets to an independent trustee. This person or firm is instructed to liquidate the assets and to distribute the proceeds among the creditors on a pro rata basis.

The procedures under Chapter 7 of the 1978 Federal Bankruptcy Reform Act achieve at least three things during a liquidation.

1. They provide a safeguard against fraud by the debtor during liquidation.

2. They provide an equitable distribution of the debtor's assets among the creditors.

3. Insolvent debtors can discharge all their obligations and start new businesses unhampered by a burden of prior debt.

Assignment has many advantages over bankruptcy. Bankruptcy is an expensive and long process. Trustees involved in assignments may be more familiar with the normal channels of trade and may be able to get better deals for the company's assets either through individual sales to other companies in the same business or through an auction. The trustees can actually act more quickly in assignments than in bankruptcies and therefore prevent the obsolescence of a firm's inventories.

THE OLD BANKRUPTCY LAW: CHAPTERS X AND XI

The original National Bankruptcy Law required that large public firms filing for bankruptcy do so under Chapter X of the code. Under Chapter

X, a firm's management was replaced with a trustee who devised an organization plan for the firm. Allocation of funds to creditors was done according to the absolute-priority rule, which stated that all senior claimants be paid in full before junior creditors received anything. To avoid these rigid, formal requirements, firms customarily attempted to file under old Chapter XI instead of Chapter X. The former was designed to be used by small nonpublic firms—usually solvent—needing protection from creditors and time to evaluate their unsecured debts and develop a repayment plan. Informal negotiations between creditors and debtor firms accelerated the reorganization process, permitting management to retain control of the firm and operations to continue. Because of the leniency with which debtor firms were treated under old Chapter XI, many public firms sought protection under the code. Although this situation offered more potential benefits for firms' shareholders than under Chapter X, it caused difficulties for its creditors in three main areas (see Schnepper, 1981).

First, secured debt and equityholders' rights were not well protected under the old Chapter XI code. Trost (1973) stated the issue very clearly in comparing proceedings under old Chapter XI and Chapter X:

Under Chapter X, any plan which provided creditors with as much or more than they would receive upon liquidation meets the statute's command that the plan must be in the "best interests" of creditors. Thus, shareholders of an insolvent Chapter XI corporation may retain an interest in the reorganized corporation even though creditors are not paid in full. But in Chapter X reorganizations the court applies a quite different rule: Unless the corporation is solvent, shareholders cannot participate in the fruits of the reorganization because of the application of the so-called absolute priority doctrine.

Second, creditors were hurt because the SEC was empowered by the courts to determine the value of a bankrupt firm. To protect shareholders from losing their investment entirely, the SEC tended to overestimate the value of the firm as a reorganized entity. Trost (1973) discussed the difficulties that resulted from this procedure:

Corporations in reorganization are valued as a going concern by capitalizing the prospective earnings of the rehabilitated corporation. Although market values, liquidation values, and past earnings records may be relevant, they are not determinative. . . . Some courts and commentators are more candid than others about the difficulties inherent in the valuation problem. . . . Particularly troublesome is the choice of the proper capitalization rate. Assuming that future earnings can somehow be forecast, a change in the capitalization rate one-half point up or down can have momentous consequences for junior interests. . . . By a slight change of the capitalization rate, an insolvent company in which shareholders are denied participation becomes a solvent company in which shareholders are entitled to some kind of interest. It seems not likely that implicit in the choice of a rate may be the desire to rationalize a predetermined result, as for instance, the retention of the common shareholders in the enterprise.

Finally, many firms wished to file under Chapter XI because management was allowed to remain in control of the operations, whereas under Chapter X they were automatically ousted. Meckling (1977) pointed out:

There are apparently occasions on which it pays creditors to concede something to shareholders in order to keep the current management. . . . It is an open question whether the managerial retention case is empirically important. As a corporation approaches insolvency, it will become more and more attractive to the stockholders to have management convert assets into cash and pay the cash out as dividends. These are constraints on what management can do to serve these interests, but such constraints cannot be fully effective. One conversion opportunity which is very difficult to monitor is the abandonment of maintenance. In the case of Penn Central, for example, it was practically impossible to tell whether the failure to maintain track beds was efficient or represented a conversion of assets into cash flow for the benefit of stockholders. Given that stockholders have such opportunities, creditors may find it desirable to concede positive shares in bankruptcy to them as a way of discouraging exploitation.

THE NEW BANKRUPTCY LAW: CHAPTER 11

Reform of the National Bankruptcy Act addressed two of the above problems creditors faced when firms filed under Chapter XI instead of Chapter X by combining the procedures of both codes into a new form of Chapter 11. Its new provisions can be summarized as follows (see Schnepper, 1981):

1. Firms do not have to demonstrate balance sheet insolvency in order to petition for reorganization, but can now file based on an inability to pay their general creditors. This amendment allows firms to file more quickly and before large-scale erosion of their financial positions occurs.
2. Management is allowed to retain control of the firm, sustain operations, and provide a return on investment for shareholders.
3. Not all reorganization plans need to adhere to the absolute-priority rule. More compromise and informal negotiation can now take place between creditors and debtors.
4. The role of the Securities and Exchange Commission in reorganizations has been expanded. To help understand the expanded role of the SEC and why the new law appears to give filing firms greater benefits than the old law, an overview of the court's procedural system follows.

The involvement of the SEC in the reorganization cases was as important under the old law as it is under the new one. However, the form of its authority has changed. The Chandler Act of 1938 provided the procedural means for the SEC to participate in bankruptcy corporate reorganization proceedings to provide protection for public investors. Under the new Chapter 11, a disclosure approach—analogous to that under the securities law—is followed in lieu of the former approach involving scrutiny and approval of a plan proposal's merits by the SEC and the court. Under the old law, the SEC had to be invited by the judge or interested parties to participate in a reorganization proceeding. Now Section 1109 (a) of Chapter 11 gives the SEC authorization to intervene at any time and be heard on any issue (see Corroto and Pickard, 1979).

In addition, Congress determined that—as under the federal securities law—the parties of interest should be given adequate information to enable them to make their own informed judgments as to whether they should accept or reject a reorganization plan. The amount of disclosure required is flexible, taking into account the facts of a particular case, and is determined by the SEC. In the interest of expediency, reorganized plans, under the new law, can be approved without an extensive investigation of the firm's financial situation.

COMPARATIVE ANALYSIS OF THE OLD AND THE NEW BANKRUPTCY LAWS

In the past, Chapter XI required that the trustee transmit to creditors, stockholders, and other interested parties a report or summary of an investigation into a firm's financial state. One purpose of that report was to provide information to those who could submit suggestions in response to the trustee's request. Under Chapter 11, the debtor submitted an arrangement that, in most cases, had been negotiated with the official creditors' committee. The new Chapter 11, however, provides that a debtor can file a plan at any time, even before an examiner's report is completed. Thus it will be difficult for other interested parties to comment on the plan since they will not have received all the information available about a debtor's financial state. In summary, it is possible that creditors and stockholders will be asked to vote on a reorganization plan having only limited information about a firm's financial state.[2]

Not only the lack of required information, but also the acceptance standards, tend to favor the adoption of management's proposed reorganization plan. Under former Chapter X the "fair and equitable" standard, otherwise known as the absolute priority rule, was one of the key public investor protection features. Since the former Chapter XI confirmation standard of "best interests of creditors" meant that a creditor received more than in liquidation, a negotiated arrangement usually worked

to retain enhanced value for the shareholders at the expense of the unsecured creditors. Thus public debenture holders, under former Chapter
XI, could receive less than their absolute priority vis-a-vis stockholders.
Considering that the debtor was the only one that could propose a plan,
creditors had to negotiate with management for a larger share of the
company. Currently, under Chapter 11, both sets of standards are applied. The key provision of the law provides that the court shall confirm
a plan if either "each class" (or claimant) has accepted or is not impaired under the plan.

The court must examine the acceptance of the plan by each impaired
class in order to determine if *each member* of the class has accepted the
plan, or, if not, whether a person rejecting the plan will receive under
the plan "not less than the amount" he or she would have received in
liquidation. An accepting class majority can bind the dissenting minority
members to a distribution differing from that which the "fair and equitable" standard would otherwise mandate as long as it is not less than
what the minority member would have received if the debtor were liquidated. This approach will have a significant impact on public classes
of debt securityholders because they will be bound to a distribution where
only two-thirds in amount and one-half in number of allowed claims of
the class actually voting can decide to accept the plan proponent's offer.
Thus the interests of a public investor class may be controlled by the
interests of the few, larger class claimants.

If a plan is rejected by one or more classes, the proponent of the plan
may request that the court still confirm the plan if it is bound to be "fair
and equitable" to each such class. The importance of adequate and effective public investor representation and participation in a reorganization case is underscored by the new act's approach to confirmation. Under former Chapter X, public investors had the independent trustee, the
SEC, and the court to ensure them of a fair and equitable participation
under the plan. Thus, they were not left to negotiate a relative participation on their own. The act now places this responsibility on the investors with a "fairness" backstop possible only if the class dissents and
the proponents elect to go forward and not withdraw.

In summary, with the Bankruptcy Reform Act of 1978, Congress
adopted a new approach to the means by which investor protections are
achieved in business reorganization of public entities. The prior focus on
the disinterested trustee, the required investigation, the independent formulation of a plan, SEC scrutiny, and court approval of the plan is now
shifted to an emphasis on investor initiative and vigilance and to the
disclosure of "adequate information" in order that the interested parties
themselves can reach informed judgments. The flexibility of former
Chapter XI and the rigidity of former Chapter X have given way to a
single reorganization Chapter 11 under which the presumption is that the

debtor generally will remain in possession. However, with disclosure of "adequate information" drawing closer to the securities laws concept than was the case under former law, debtor control of plan formulation and confirmation will have to be balanced against the protection of investors. SEC participation in the disclosure process and prior court approval of the disclosure statement are two important investor protection features designed to assure continued investor protection.

One additional problem that the new law does not address is the valuation of a reorganizing firm by the SEC and the reliance of the court on this estimate of firm value. Meckling (1977) expresses his concern with the law's revisions when he states:

In particular, the revisions would significantly soften rigid adherence to absolute priority in settlement claims under Chapter X. This will tend to give shareholders in publicly held corporations more power in bankruptcy than they currently possess. Meanwhile the revisions more or less ignore the problem of valuation of a firm. . . . As a result of intensive research over the last decade or so, we now know a great deal about how the value of firms is determined in financial markets. Most of us would have little faith that estimates derived by the SEC staff would be superior to those that markets would generate.

As the new code has been in effect only a short while, no consensus exists in the literature as to whether the new law is more efficient than the one it replaced. The current opinion of some bankruptcy experts (see Altman, 1983b) is that, on balance, the new law is easier to apply and less costly for all involved.

Lack of data and confounding economic variables make any empirical comparison of the old law versus the new code extremely nebulous. For example, Dun and Bradstreet's 1987 Failure Record reported that the number of firms filing for new Chapter 11 protection rose since the law became effective in 1979. The reasons for this dramatic increase in firm failures may have been totally unrelated to the law's revision. Instead, high interest rates, a long persistent recession, and climbing debt ratios may have been the principal culprits. Given this conflict, the goal of an investor is not to determine if investors were better off investing in firms that filed under the old law. Instead, the implications of the new law should be taken as the legal environment in which all Chapter 11 firms must operate. The importance of the law for investment analysis of bankruptcy stocks is:

1. The law allows distressed firms the opportunity to file quickly and halt basic deterioration of their capital structures. It seems evident that the more quickly they were able to file and start reorganization proceedings the more likely they were to emerge successfully from Chapter 11.

2. There seems to be a significant difference in bankruptcy costs under the old versus the new law. White (1983) argues that aggregate bankruptcy costs are lower under the new law. If market efficiency holds for Chapter 11 securities, the effect of these lower costs should be incorporated into their prices. If market participants are unaware of these cost changes or, if aware, are uncertain as to their measurement, then prices of Chapter 11 firms may not reflect their true values. They may be too low.

In conclusion, although the new Chapter 11 law attempts to correct some of the delays in resolution of bankruptcy cases, it appears to provide less protection for creditors. In addition, new shareholders of a newly reorganized firm may be able to earn positive excess returns, which are simply the reflection of negative abnormal returns to other claimants.

NOTES

1. This section and the sections on out-of-court settlements, court-directed involuntary settlements, and liquidation are based on Chapter 31 of Weston and Copeland (1986).

2. Since the appointment of trustees is not required under the new law, the court sometimes appoints an examiner to investigate a debtor firm. The court decides on a case-by-case basis the nature and extent of the investigation. Also, it may not be necessary for the court to consider the report of an examiner before the reorganization can proceed.

Prediction of Successful
Reorganization

As discussed in Chapter 2, shrewd investors in bankrupt firms are likely
to obtain above-average (higher than S&P 500) returns. The returns would
be higher to the person who invests only in firms that are likely to be
reorganiized after filing for bankruptcy. Predicting successful reorganization thus becomes a very profitable endeavor.

Since the 1978 Bankruptcy Reform Act became law, many financially
distressed firms have rushed to file for court protection of their assets.
This trend is partly because the new law has made it easier and less
traumatic for management to file for Chapter 11. Managements no longer
need to prove that their firms are insolvent. In response to this change
in the operational features of a Chapter 11 filing, investors have become
speculators in the market for reorganizing firms' financial securities. They
are buying the stocks and bonds of these firms, immediately after a filing
takes place, in the hopes of receiving large capital gains.

INVESTMENT RISK

Those who invest in bankrupt firms with the expectation of reaping
rich rewards when the firms reorganize (emerge from bankruptcy) also
bear unusual risks, which are those associated with the reorganization
of the bankrupt firm. Any attempt to identify firm-related factors that
indicate a high probability of reorganization would thus prove to be ben-
eficial to the investor.

Publicly available information regarding the bankrupt firm is, at best,

scant. During the reorganization process firms often do not publish annual reports or any financial information. Most firms no longer trade on
an organized exchange, or if they do, trading is infrequent. Also large
institutional traders sell or abandon their holdings of Chapter 11 stocks.
Thus the stocks of bankrupt firms become illiquid. Reorganization risk
results from the uncertainty surrounding bankruptcy, such as judicial
factors that are beyond the control of management. One of the elements
in reorganization risk is negotiation among creditors, managers, and
shareholders searching for an acceptable compromise that will not result
in the liquidation of the assets of the firm. Another factor is uncertainty
about how the courts will apply the new law to each firm's situation.
The unresolved question during a court-supervised reorganization is, "Who
will benefit the most: creditors, shareholders, or some other constitu-
ent?" The uncertainty surrounding the distribution of the wealth of a
firm will affect the way individual investors perceive the risk of the firm.

However, not all investors of reorganizing companies believe that a
firm's risk will increase after filing. The reorganization process could
reduce the firm-specific risk of the filing firms. Firm-specific risk is defined as the risk arising from factors that are characteristic to a particular
company or industry. Court protection from creditor debts could reduce
firm-specific risk as it helps strengthen a firm's financial position. Also a
decline in specific risk can be expected if higher earnings potential exists
after filing because of a lighter debt load, or if management changes the
thrust of its investment policies to include less risky projects.

Despite the increased risk of investing in bankrupt firms, do investors
earn excess risk-adjusted returns purchasing these equities after the
companies have filed for reorganization? Can a model be developed that
could be used by investors who are interested in purchasing such stocks?
The model presented in this chapter is designed to identify factors that
will predict successful reorganization.

The model is based on after-filing return and risk characteristics of
Chapter 11 firms. While chapter 2 of this book tested for excess market
returns in a portfolio consisting of bankrupt firms, this chapter looks into
the possibility of predicting bankrupt companies that have a high probability of being reorganized. In the least, attempt is made to identify the
factors that play a role in the reorganization of bankrupt firms.

POST-BANKRUPTCY PERFORMANCE OF BANKRUPT FIRMS

Most of the extant literature on the performance of bankrupt firms
deals with the effect on the firm under the old Chapter X law of bankruptcy. Moreover, most studies also constrain themselves to explaining
the performance *prior* to bankruptcy. Most reorganizing firms were viewed
as losers not deserving investigation.

One of the first researchers to study the returns to shareholders from holding shares in bankrupt companies was Altman (1969). For the time period 1941–65, he showed that common stockholders of a bankrupt firm tended to earn as much return as all other equityholders of the New York Stock Exchange stocks if the reorganized firm survived at least five years after its filing date. His advice to investors was "to determine which firms are likely candidates for a successful reorganization and then wait at least one month after the petition date to purchase the security." As reported in chapter 2, for the period October 1, 1979, to December 31, 1983, the average annualized return on firms that successfully achieved reorganization and emerged as a single entity or as part of another firm was 49%. Over the same period the S&P 500 achieved an annualized return of 15.8%. Clearly, an ability to predict or even strongly suspect successful reorganization of a bankrupt firm could be information worth possessing to an investor in the stock market.

The ability to distinguish bankrupt firms that are likely to reorganize from firms that are destined to liquidate is crucial. The average annualized returns for the sample of 50 bankrupt firms mentioned in chapter 2 ranged from a positive 348% to a 100% loss in value! Currently a new set of studies has sought to discriminate between reorganized and liquidated firms in bankruptcy. Casey, McGee, and Stickney (1986) empirically studied this issue. Using probit analysis, these researchers tested a model that was proposed by M. White (1981, 1984) for distinguishing between firms that successfully reorganize from those that liquidate. The results of their analysis indicate that the proportion of assets not secured or pledged at the bankruptcy filing date and the change in profitability in the years preceding bankruptcy were the most important factors in predicting reorganization. Their model had a 58.5% accuracy rate in classifying firms as reorganized or liquidated.

PROBABILISTIC MODEL OF SUCCESSFUL REORGANIZATION

The data sample for this model included those firms that filed Chapter 11 petitions for reorganization after the new law became effective on October 1, 1979, and survived for at least a year after filing. A sample of 50 firms was selected from a list of the approximately 200 firms that filed for Chapter 11 between October 1, 1979, and December 31, 1982. This list was obtained from the Corporate Reorganization Department of the SEC. We chose sample companies from the population of Chapter 11 firms using the following criteria:

1. Monthly and daily return or price data were available publicly (data sources and greater description of this data item are in chapter 2).

2. Financial information on a firm was obtainable from *Moody's Industrial Manuals* just prior to filing.

The Valuation Logit Model

Only recently (see Casey et al., 1986; and Hong, 1983) have studies begun to focus on the outcome of a bankruptcy filing by a firm. Hong (1983) hypothesized that the difference between the value of the firm as a going concern and its value in liquidation would be the major explanatory factor affecting eventual outcome. Based on White's [1981, 1984] model, Casey et al. demonstrated that the significant variables that discriminate between firms that reorganize and those that liquidate are the "free assets" (noncollateralized, unencumbered assets) and change in profitability in the years preceding bankruptcy. The choice of explanatory variables in this study is guided by the above studies and others.

The following is a list of some of the factors from White's model used by Casey et al.:

1. Amount of unsecured assets.
2. Size measured by total assets.
3. Change in size from three years before filing to filing.
4. Earning prospects measured by net income divided by total assets.
5. Earning prospects measured by retained earnings divided by total assets.
6. Equity commitment of management measured by stock options available for managers.

Their results indicated that only the amount of unsecured assets and earnings prospects affected whether a firm reorganized or liquidated.

Our probabilistic model attempts to predict, based on the variables affecting the value of a firm at the time of bankruptcy filing, whether a firm will or will not reorganize. Banz (1981) was one of the first researchers who established the existence of a small firm effect. He found that investors in small firms could earn abnormal returns because the market underestimated the risk and analysts had little financial information on the firms. In subsequent research, Arbel, Carvell, and Strebel (1983) studied firms neglected by analysts. They discovered that superior return performance was obtained by the neglected firms in their sample compared to the smaller firms. Since reorganizing firms are often neglected by analysts, it is possible their performance will match those in the Arbel et al. study. We incorporated size into our analysis, since we were interested in testing White's hypothesis that larger firms are more likely to reorganize than smaller firms.

Many researchers (Solomon, 1963; Miller and Modigliani, 1966; Gordon, 1962; and Graham, 1962) have argued that growth is a major factor in determining a firm's value. Thus, we incorporated the growth factor of a Chapter 11 firm in our model. As a surrogate for an individual firm's growth rate, we used the firm's industry growth rate, because there is a body of literature that provides evidence that the industry in which a firm is a member affects its value (see Reilly and Drzyciemski, 1974; Livingston, 1977; King, 1960; and Meyers, 1973). Since growth during the reorganization process is not hampered by required dividend payments, all income is reinvested in a Chapter 11 firm. It is possible that court protection reduces the risk of a firm to the point that its expected growth rate is greater than the required rate of return demanded by investors. Using Gordon's (1962) model:

$$P = \frac{D_1}{K_e - g} \tag{1}$$

where

P = expected price of a stock

D_1 = expected dividend

K_e = expected required rate of return

g = expected growth rate.

If K_e is less than g the price or value of a stock will converge to infinity. Growth is, thus, an important factor in determining stock value.

Finally, we incorporated into the logit model the amount of debt a firm holds at filing in relation to its equity value. Beaver (1968b) showed that the ratio of total debt to equity helps creditors predict bankruptcy of the firm. It is reasonable to assume that the amount of debt a firm holds will impact on its ability to reorganize successfully.

Data

The source of data for the probabilistic logit model is *Moody's Industrial Manuals* for information on a firm's assets, age, and debt ratio at the time of filing.

Growth rate of the industry (of the bankrupt firm) relative to the rest of the economy is derived from production statistics published in various issues of *The Federal Reserve Bulletin*. These growth rates are estimated as averages for the post-bankruptcy period up to reorganization or liquidation as the case may be. Corporate bond monthly total returns are obtained from the Center for Research in Security Prices index files containing Ibbotson-Sinquefield estimated long-term corporate bond monthly total returns.

Methodology

Three significant dates are referred to in this chapter: the filing date, when a firm files for bankruptcy; the reorganization date, when the bankrupt firm's reorganization plan is approved; and the liquidation date, when the bankruptcy court converts reorganization proceedings into liquidation proceedings. Figure 5.1 illustrates these dates.

It is hypothesized that the market value of the bankrupt firm at each point in time, *t*, determines whether it will be reorganized or liquidated. At time *t*, if the value of the assets, if liquidated, is greater than the present value of the firm if reorganized, then the bankrupt firm will be liquidated. There is no well-accepted theory to guide the selection of variables that determine the value of a bankrupt firm. However, based on the results of the previously mentioned empirical studies, the follow-

Figure 5.1
Relevant Dates for Reorganization of a Firm

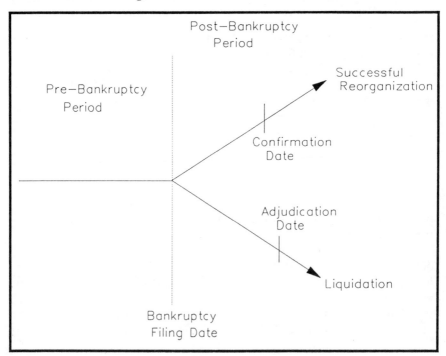

ing valuation choice model is posited for bankrupt firms awaiting reorganization.

The market value of a bankrupt firm (V) to an investor (creditor) is a function of the expected outcome of bankruptcy proceedings. Let V_1 be the expected value of the assets of the firm if liquidated. The market value of the assets will be determined by the growth of the industry (of the bankrupt firm) relative to the rest of the economy. This assumption is guided by the fact that a firm in a sunset industry is not likely to possess assets that are very valuable at the time of liquidation. The value of the assets are also determined by its age. Let V_r be the expected value of free, uncommitted assets (i.e., assets minus debts) of the firm, if reorganized. This value is likely to be a function of the potential growth and attractiveness of the industry and firm assets. As such, the growth rate of the industry relative to the rest of the economy, and the age of the firm up to bankruptcy date, are determinants of the firm value. The latter variable is also a proxy for experience of the management, which is so crucial for the future survival of the firm. Value of the reorganized firm is offset by the opportunity cost to the creditor in letting debt remain in the firm. Since opportunity cost will be affected by the general state of the economy, monthly total return on long-term corporate bonds is used as a proxy for this variable. We should thus expect the sign of this coefficient to be negative. Thus at time t,

if $V_1 < V_r$, then the firm will be reorganized, and

if $V_1 > V_r$, then the firm will be liquidated.

As discussed above, let

$$V_1 = f(ASSETS_{t_b}, RELGRTH_{t_b, t_1}, AGE_{t_b}) \tag{2}$$

$$V_r = f(FREE\ ASSETS_{t_b}, RELGRTH_{t_b, t_r}, CBTR_{t_r}, AGE_{t_b}) \tag{3}$$

where
$ASSETS_{t_b}$ = Total assets at the bankruptcy filing date

$FREE ASSETS_{t_b}$ = Total (assets-debts) at the bankruptcy filing date

$RELGRTH_{t_b, t_1}$ = Growth rate of the industry relative to the entire manufacturing sector between the filing and the liquidation date

$RELGRTH_{t_b, t_r}$ = Growth rate of the industry relative to the entire manufacturing sector between filing and reorganization date

AGE_{t_b} = Age of the firm up to the bankruptcy filing date

$CBTR_{t_r}$ = Monthly total return on longterm corporate bond

Assuming a linear functional form (homogeneous of degree one) for equations 2 and 3,

$$V_1 = i_1 + a_1 \cdot ASSETS + b_1 \cdot RELGRTH + c_1 \cdot AGE + \epsilon_1 \text{ and} \tag{4}$$

$$V_r = i_r + f \cdot (ASSETS - DEBTS) + b_r \cdot RELGRTH + c_r \cdot AGE + g \cdot CBTR + \epsilon_r \tag{5}$$

Assuming ϵ_1 and ϵ_r are identically and independently distributed with the standard extreme value cumulative distribution, a logit model is constructed (see McFadden 1974), where

$$\mathrm{Log}\left(\frac{P}{1-P}\right) = i + a \cdot ASSETS + f \cdot DEBTS + b \cdot RELGRTH + c \cdot AGE + \\ g \cdot CBTR + (\epsilon_r - \epsilon_1) \tag{6}$$

where
$P =$ Probability that a bankrupt firm will be reorganized.
$a = f - a_1$
$i = i_r - i_1$
$b = b_r - b_1$
$c = c_r - c_1$

Thus, a logistic regression of the probability of reorganization of a bankrupt firm against the independent variables given in equation 6 would yield the values of the coefficients. We expect the coefficients f and g to be negative in sign. Care should be exercised in interpreting these coefficients. As parameters of the valuation model (equations 4 and 5), these coefficients can be interpreted as incremental effects of the independent variables on the liquidation or reorganization values of bankrupt firms. Furthermore, as shown in the next section, these coefficients provide insights regarding the odds of reorganization of a bankrupt firm.

Results and Analysis

The three explanatory variables that have a significant effect on the probability of reorganization of a bankrupt firm are the total assets and debts at the time of bankruptcy and the relative growth rate of the industry vis-a-vis the manufacturing sector in the post-bankruptcy period. The significance of the assets and debts bears out previous findings (refer to Casey et al., 1986) that net, unencumbered assets ("free assets") is a significant variable in discriminating between firms that organize and firms that liquidate.

Additionally, our model points to the importance of the relative growth rate of the industry of the bankrupt firm in the post-bankruptcy period in determining the probability of survival of the firm.

Table 5.1 contains the values of the logit model coefficients. These results also indicate that an increase in the debt by $1 million hurts the odds of reorganization more than an increase in the assets by the same

Table 5.1
Probability of Reorganization: Logistic Regression Parameters

Events or Independent Variables	Response Variable (Probability of reorganization)	
	Parameter Estimates (1)	Incremental Effect on Probability of Reorganization (2)*
	(Chi—squares are given in parentheses)	
Intercept	0.57359	0.1434
	(0.35)	
ASSETS	0.05679	0.0142
(in millions of dollars)	(2.03)	
DEBTS	-0.00896	-0.0022
(in thousands of dollars)	(1.74)	
RELGRTH	0.00469	0.0012
	(2.39)	
AGE	-0.0253	-0.0063
	(0.55)	
CBTR	-0.1761	-0.0440
(Monthly total return)	(1.19)	

Note: * Please refer to the text; incremental probability of reorganization, P ~ (Col.1) * [P (1-P)] and assuming P = 0.5, (Col.2) = (Col.1)*0.25.

amount would aid the odds. Interestingly, relative growth rate of the industry in the post-bankruptcy period aids the probability of reorganization more than it aids the probability of liquidation of the bankrupt firm. As expected, an increase in the corporate bond return (opportunity cost of alternative investment to the creditor) adversely affects the odds of reorganization in favor of liquidation. Age of the firm, used as a proxy for management experience, does not significantly affect the odds of reorganization. It is as if, once the firm files for bankruptcy, the investor community loses its confidence in the existing management and the firm's history is irrelevant for determining the odds of reorganization.

The effect of a change in the independent variables on the probability of reorganization, P, can easily be shown to be[1]:

$$P = \text{Regression Parameter Estimate} * [P(1-P)] \tag{7}$$

Assuming a 50–50 odds of reorganization (i.e., $P=0.5$), column 2 of Table 5.1 indicates the incremental effect of the independent variables on the probability of reorganization. Keeping in mind the level of significance of the independent variables (this is indicated by the value of the Chi-square in parentheses), for a firm with an even chance of reorganization ($P = 0.5$) a decrease of 0.25% in the monthly corporate bond rate (or about 3% annual rate) increases the probability of reorganization by as much as an increase in the assets by $1 million. This highlights the importance of the overall economic climate as much as the firm specific variables in assessing the probability of reorganization of a bankrupt firm.

The predictive nature of the model was tested by determining the probability of reorganization on a hold-out sample of eight firms that had not reorganized as of December 1985.[2] The five firms that have high probability of reorganization, according to our model, are HRT, Manville, UNR, FSC, and Nucorp.

UNR, formerly the United Asbestos and Rubber Company, filed for Chapter 11 protection on July 29, 1982. Its steel operations, which accounted for most of its sales, left UNR unable to cope with asbestos litigation expenses that exceeded $1 million a month. The UNR reorganization plan will leave a trust fund for asbestos victims in control of a majority of the company's stock—about 64%. Creditors must vote on the plan by May 1, 1989, and it is expected to be confirmed after a hearing scheduled for May 31, 1989. The Manville reorganization plan, approved in November 1988, created a $2.5 billion trust fund to compensate personal-injury victims and a second trust to pay property damage claims to schools, hospitals, and businesses now forced to remove asbestos. The trust funds control a majority of Manville's stock and will have access, if necessary, to 20% of its future profits. All claims must be filed against the trusts. While HRT and FSC had been bought out, Nucorp Energy Corporation was liquidated with its officers sued for fraud. HRT became a subsidiary of McCrory Corporation while FSC (Funding Systems Corporation) became a subsidiary of The Bank of Boston.

SUMMARY

The rewards of investing in bankrupt firms are substantial. During the period of our study (1979–83) an investor in a portfolio of bankrupt firms could have earned an average of 50% annual return compared to an average of about 16% for the S&P 500 market portfolio for the same period. However, as is to be expected, the risks also are substantial. The range of returns of the bankrupt portfolio ranged from a +350% to a −100%, suggesting scope for substantial loss arising from an inappropriate choice of bankrupt firms.

Some recent studies have attempted to address the issue of predictability of reorganization of firms that file for bankruptcy. These studies have tried to identify the factors that seem to influence the probability of eventual reorganization. Our research is of the same nature.

While previous studies found the presence of free, unencumbered assets as the important determinant of the probability of reorganization, we have been able to identify additional economic variables of equal importance. We used a probabilistic logit model to estimate the influence of economic and firm-specific variables on the ultimate probability of reorganization. The logit parameters of our valuation model confirm the importance of total assets and debts ("free assets") in the estimation of reorganization probabilities of bankrupt firms. Additionally, the overall economic climate (relative importance of the industry in which the bankrupt firm is located and the economic opportunity cost to investors represented by the total return on corporate bonds) as much as the firm-specific variables are shown to be important in the assessment of reorganization probability. Finally, the predictive ability of the model is tested by estimating the probability of reorganization of a hold-out sample of eight firms which had not reorganized or liquidated as of December 1985.

NOTES

1. See Pindyck and Rubinfeld (1981, p. 229).
2. A measure of goodness-of-fit analogous to R^2 was estimated for the logit model. The estimated R^2 is 0.3862. See Pindyck and Rubinfeld (1981, p. 312).

Stock Market Efficiency and Bankrupt Firms

Much has been written about the efficiency of the stock market. It would aid our discussion of market efficiency with respect to bankrupt firms if we were to begin with a precise definition of market efficiency.

MARKET EFFICIENCY

Definition

The notion of capital market efficiency is closely related to the effectiveness with which the market processes information. In an efficient capital market, prices of securities fully and instantaneously reflect all available relevant information.[1] In such a market if all the available information regarding a security were to be revealed to the public there would be no change in the price of that security. This presupposes simultaneous awareness of all relevant information by all the individuals participating in the market. A practical implication of this is the assumption of a random walk process as being descriptive of the stock market returns. (Please see the section on "Stock Market Analysis and the Bankrupt Firm" explained below.)

Efficient capital markets need not be perfect capital markets. The latter describes a more restrictive market form and is used only as a benchmark paradigm. Perfect capital markets require frictionless (no transaction costs or taxes) markets, perfect competition in product and securities markets, costless information, and rational expected utility maximizing participants. Since security prices can fully reflect all available information even in the presence of transaction costs, taxes, costly information, or imperfect competition in the product markets, capital markets can be efficient but imperfect.

The more common notion of allocational efficiency in the capital markets dealing with transfer of funds between savers and borrowers requires that financial assets be priced to reflect their marginal returns (adjusted for risk). In equilibrium these returns will be equal for buyers and sellers. To the extent that information affecting the expected return from buying (or selling) an asset is not reflected in the asset price, the market is not efficient in the above sense. Thus, allocational efficiency requires informational efficiency.

Economists (Fama, 1970, 1976) have operationalized the notion of capital market efficiency into three types of efficiency. These types are based on the nature of information that are incorporated in the price of the security. A weak-form efficiency obtains when historical price or return information does not provide trading rules that could result in achieving excess returns. A semistrong form efficiency exists when publicly available information (company annual reports, business publications, etc.) are inadequate in generating trading rules that could achieve excess returns. Strong form efficiency forbids achieving excess returns using any information, whether publicly available or not. This last form implies existence of no special advantage to possession of inside corporate information.

Market Prescience

It is recognized that the stock market makes rational forecasts of the economy. This is especially true of the real sector (real GNP, physical productivity of investments, etc.). For example, bull markets normally seem to begin during recessions (leading the trough of business activity, on the average, by five months) rather than during economic growth, and bear markets seem to lead the peak of economic expansions, on the average, by ten months (see Tables 6.1 and 6.2).

In recognition of this property of the stock market, it has been included as one of the 12 indicators of the composite leading indicators of the economy published monthly by the Commerce Department. A legitimate question to ask here is, How far into the future does the market foresee and does it distinguish the supply and demand forces of the economy? In other words, do anticipated changes in the demand and supply factors of the economy that are equally far into the future have comparable effects on the stock market today?

At a micro level, the ability of the market to integrate all available information (the past, the present, and the future) pertaining to a secu-

Table 6.1
Bull Markets and Recessions

Date of Bull Market Beginning (S&P 500)	Date of Trough in Economy	Number of Months Market Trough Led Economic Trough
September 1953	May 1954	8
December 1957	April 1958	4
October 1960	February 1961	4
June 1970	November 1970	5
October 1974	March 1975	5
July 1982	November 1982	4
Average		5

Source: *Business Conditions Digest*, U.S. Department of Commerce, Bureau of Economic Analysis, Washington, D.C. April 1988, p.105.

Table 6.2
Bear Markets and Expansions

Date of Bear Market Beginning (S&P 500)	Date of Peak in Economy	Number of Months Market Peak Led Economic Peak
January 1953	July 1953	6
July 1956	August 1957	13
July 1959	April 1960	9
December 1968	December 1969	12
January 1973	November 1973	10
November 1980	July 1981	8
Average		10

Source: *Business Conditions Digest*, U.S. Department of Commerce, Bureau of Economic Analysis, Washington, D.C. April 1988, p.105.

rity enables it to anticipate the future financial health of a firm. Since security prices reflect the forecasted potential of a firm, an intriguing question to formulate would be to ask how early the market foresees the impending bankruptcy of a firm.

In the next two sections we will investigate the forecasting ability of the stock market as it relates to the economy as a whole and specifically to financially troubled firms. Stock market perception of future economic decline ought to forewarn the existence of a generally hostile environment for financially weak firms while the firm-specific forecasts help to identify the most probable candidates for bankruptcy. Additionally, any difference in the manner in which the stock market takes its cues of the future from the economic demand-and-supply-related factors will establish the effect of the orientation of public policy on the current state of the market. Such research ought to offer answers to questions of whether public policy seeking to influence the current state of the stock market should be focused on short-term demand factors or long-term supply factors.

THE STOCK MARKET AND THE ECONOMY

It is well accepted that the stock market makes rational forecasts of the real sector. Fama (1981) has shown that the rate of growth in the next period's real GNP explains a significant amount of current period stock price variation. Breeden, (1979) in his seminal paper on equilibrium asset pricing, argues that the current value of an asset depends on investment opportunity (physical productivity of investments) in future states of the world. Grossman and Shiller (1981), using a lifetime consumption model, show that the expected return of an asset depends on the covariance of the asset's return with the marginal rate of substitution between current and future consumption. This concept is very similar to Breeden's "consumption beta."

In the next section, we model real common stock return as a function of the risk attitude of the economy and supply-and-demand forces affecting future levels of economic activity.

Model

The role of a firm in the traditional intertemporal consumption-investment analysis is to provide the opportunity for deferred consumption (i.e., investment). Viewed thus, real common stock return in such a firm is determined by real price changes of consumption goods in the economy. Asset returns are thus affected by both the demand and supply forces affecting consumption goods in the economy (Breeden, 1980). Expected future aggregate demand and productivity are two proxies for the economy-wide demand and supply forces affecting future consumption. (Productivity could also be viewed as a proxy for investment opportunity in a given state.[2]) Next, as Grossman and Shiller (1981) have argued, marginal rate of substitution between current and future consumption is yet another important determinant of expected asset return, since it provides information on the appropriate discount rate to be applied to future earnings stream from an asset.

Real common stock returns are thus viewed as a function of information on future aggregate demand and supply forces affecting future consumption and the economy's risk attitude as evidenced by the marginal rate of substitution (MRS) between current and future consumption. Hence,

$$RCSR_t = a + b \cdot RGNP_{t+k} + c \cdot TFPY_{t+k} + d \cdot MRS_{t,t+k} + \epsilon_t \qquad (1)$$

where

k $= 1,2,3, \ldots$

$RCSR_t$ = Ex-ante real common stock return of a market portfolio

$RGNP_{t+k}$ = Ex-ante (at time t) expected real GNP at time $t+k$

$TFPY_{t+k}$ = Ex-ante expected total factor productivity at time $t+k$

$MRS_{t,t+k}$ = Expected marginal rate of substitution between consumption at time t and $t+k$ (this is explained below)

ϵ_t = Error term

Let the reciprocal of the usual measure of marginal rate of substitution between present and future consumption in a one-period model be

$$MRS_{t,t+1} = a \, \frac{U'(C_{t+1})}{U'(C_t)}$$
$$= a \, \frac{\partial C_t}{\partial C_{t+1}} \qquad (2)$$

where

$U'(C)$ = Marginal utility of consumption

a $= \dfrac{1}{1+r}$

r = Subjective rate of time preference

A necessary condition for optimal asset holdings at time t, given that the consumer maximizes expected value of a stream of present discounted value of utilities of consumption, is:[3]

$$E(RCSR_t \cdot MRS_{t,t+1}) = 1 \qquad (3)$$

$$E(RCSR_t) = E(MRS_{t,t+1})^{-1} \cdot (1 - cov[R_t \cdot MRS_{t,t+1}]) \tag{4}$$

In equation 1 asset prices are determined by two opposing forces: aggregate demand of the economy exerting an upward pressure on asset prices and productivity (representing potential aggregate supply or investment opportunity) exerting a downward pressure. We should expect higher current real return on the market portfolio, the higher the expected future real GNP. Similarly, the larger the anticipated future real supply (productivity), the smaller the expected real stock return. In the context of the Breeden model, this is tantamount to characterizing a future state of the economy as abounding in investment opportunity. An asset that provides a payoff in such a state is more valuable. Ex-ante expected return for such an asset will decrease. From equations 3 and 4, asset returns that come in periods of low marginal utility of consumption (i.e., when consumption is high) are less valuable because they add little to an already large utility. Equation 4 states that the expected return of an asset depends on the covariance of the asset's return with the marginal rate of substitution. The asset is considered very "risky" if its payoff has a high negative covariance with the MRS. (This is Breeden's consumption beta.) Thus, the coefficient of $RGNP_{t+k}$ is expected to be positive while that of $TFPY_{t+k}$ and $MRS_{t,t+k}$ is negative in sign.

Data

Equation 1 requires use of ex-ante expectational data, which are hard to come by, especially as an extended time series. The Conference Board's *Statistical Bulletin* contains real GNP forecasts of half a dozen forecasters. However, the forecasts do not go back far enough (earliest available data are for 1977). Productivity forecasts are scarcer still. Again, The Conference Board's *Economic Overview* contains worldwide productivity forecasts gathered from some 350 business economists. However, the earliest available data are for 1980–81. As other researchers have noted before, we are thus left with the less-than-desirable alternative of having to use actual growth rates of future real activity and productivity instead of the anticipated rates. Results reported below are thus obtained using actual instead of anticipated rates for the period 1947–82. Real GNP and personal consumption expenditures are obtained from *Economic Report of the President–1983*. Productivity measures are from Kendrick's (1961) NBER study and from Kendrick and Grossman (1980). Total common stock returns, U.S. treasury bill rates, and inflation rates are from the Ibbotson-Sinquefield study (1979).

Results and Analysis

Table 6.3 gives summary statistics of the variables used in equation 1. The real stock return, $RCSR_t$, is the annual nominal total return (inclu-

Table 6.3
Summary Statistics of Variables, 1947–82

Variable	P_1	P_2	P_3	P_4	P_5	Mean	Std. Dev	DW
$RCSR_t$	-.16	-.19	-.14	.42*	.21	0.08	0.19	2.05
$RGNP_t$	.93*	-.05	.00	-.04	.00	946.10	331.90	0.01
$DRGNP_t$	.08	-.07	-.25	-.03	.03	0.03	0.03	1.69
$TFPY_t$	.91*	-.02	-.03	.10	.06	87.80	18.50	0.02
$DTFPY_t$	.05	-.07	-.04	.15	.09	0.02	0.02	1.84
PCE_t	.93*	-.02	.01	-.01	-.03	583.00	213.00	0.01
$DPCE_t$	.15	-.14	-.02	.03	.05	0.033	0.018	1.69
$MRS_{t,t+1}$	.34*	-.27	.33	-.11	.13	0.976	0.027	0.88

sive of dividends) on a value-weighted portfolio of all New York and American Stock Exchange common stocks less the annual inflation rates computed from the U.S. Consumer Price Index. $RGNP_t$ and $TFPY_t$ are the annual real GNP and total factor productivity indexes (private domestic business economy), respectively. Measures of marginal rate of substitution, $MRS_{t,t+k}$, are computed as outlined in equation 2. Values for (C_t/C_{t+k}) are obtained from regression equations run on the personal consumption expenditure time series PCE_t for the period 1926–83. Subjective rate of time preference, r, needed to compute $MRS_{t,t+k}$ is assumed to be equal to the real rate of return on U.S. Treasury bills. Autocorrelations significant at 95% level of confidence are identified with an asterisk.

All the level variables ($RGNP_t$, PCE_t, and $MRS_{t,t+1}$) have autocorrelations of at least the first order. Even $RCSR_t$ appears to have a significant fourth-order autocorrelation. As expected, growth rates of level variables (e.g., $DRGNP_t$, $DTFPY_t$, etc.) are free of the autocorrelation.

Equation 1 is now estimated using the data described above. Table 6.4 summarizes regression results of variations (models) of equation 1. These are the maximum likelihood estimators (MLEs) of regressions and are corrected for significant autocorrelations. All four models have anticipated signs for their regression coefficients.[4] Model 1 indicates lack of information in the contemporaneous variables, $RGNP_t$ and $TFPY_t$, for the $RSCR_t$ generation process. These findings are consistent with Fama (1981), where the only variable contemporaneously related to $RCSR_t$ was found to be the growth rate of industrial production. In all the models the significant supply-side variable, total factor productivity ($TFPY$), always appears to be of a longer lead time than the demand-related variable, real GNP ($RGNP$). Perhaps the stock market adopts a longer term view of the supply side of the economy in relation to the demand side. This is understandable as the economy's short-term supply elasticities are generally lower than the demand elasticities. Model 2 (most accept-

Table 6.4
MLE Regression Estimates on Real Common Stock Returns, 1947–82

	(t- values are given in brackets)			
	Dependent Variable : $RCSR_t$			
	Models			
	(1)	(2)	(3)	(4)
Intercept	4.33	4.23	3.78	3.83
	(2.29)	(4.62)	(5.48)	(5.78)
$RGNP_t$	7.9E-04			
	(1.26)			
$TFPY_t$	-1.6E-02			
	(-1.68)			
$MRS_{t,t+1}$	-3.58	-3.36	-3.07	-3.12
	(-2.13)	(-4.47)	(-5.6)	(-5.76)
$RGNP_{t+1}$		7.6E-04		3.1E-04
		(1.72)		(1.12)
$TFPY_{t+2}$		-1.7E-02		
		(-2.46)		
$TFPY_{t+3}$			-1.1E-02	-1.1E-02
			(-2.04)	(-2.43)
$RGNP_{t+2}$			3.0E-04	
			(0.938)	
R^2:	0.4	0.53	0.68	0.68
Durbin Watson:	3.06	2.96	2.58	2.59
Estimates corrected for:	AR(2)	AR(2)	AR(1),AR(2)	AR(1),AR(2)

Note: AR(1) and AR(2) are autocorrelations of first and second order.

able of the models presented in Table 6.4) indicates that the current year's expected stock return impounds information on next year's real GNP and total factor productivity two years hence. In all the models, the most consistently significant variable is the marginal rate of substitution between the current and next year's (or, at most, two years hence) consumption. Clearly, the value of an asset is crucially dependent on the covariance of its future payoffs with the economy's anticipated future consumption stream. Our data reveal that the foresight of the market extends up to two years into the future.

The stock market appears to look ahead by only a year while forming an expectation regarding the demand side of the economy; it looks farther ahead (two years at least) while assessing the supply side of the economy. Intuitively, this is appealing. Given the government emphasis on demand management policies in the last three decades, the stock market

Table 6.5
Real Common Stock Returns and Changes in Real Activity, 1947–82

	(t–values are given in parentheses)	
	Dependent Variable : RCSR$_t$	
	Model	
	(1)	(2)
Intercept	0.13	2.61
	(2.30)	(3.13)
DRGNP$_{t+1}$	1.38	1.49
	(1.73)	(1.95)
DPROY$_{t+2}$	-3.52	
	(-2.05)	
DMRS$_{t,t+1}$	-1.04	
	(-1.41)	
TFPY$_{t+2}$		-5.2E-03
		(-2.79)
MRS$_{t,t+1}$		-2.14
		(-2.79)
R^2	0.25	0.36
Durbin Watson:	1.6	1.98

has come to expect rapid changes in the demand forces of the economy. This makes a short-term view of the economy appropriate. At the same time, the neglect of supply-oriented policies (the data set used for this study is from 1947 to 1982) and the significance of supply elasticities over a longer time frame argue for adoption of a longer term view to assess the supply-side responses of the economy. The stock market appears to do just that. *MRS* between current and future consumption is significant when the future refers to at most two years. Perhaps, in the aggregate, the economy is more risk-averse than risk-neutral. This follows from equations 2 and 3.

Fama (1981) argues that the less-autocorrelated differences in variables represent new information. As such, in a rational expectations world, stock market returns should respond to rates of growth in these variables. He finds stock market returns leading all the real variables and, in particular, rate of growth of real GNP. This, he posits, is evidence of stock market utilizing the earliest information on the capital investment process. In Table 6.5, we test for a similar information-related effect of innovations (differences) in the explanatory variables on market return.

From Table 6.3 we see that all the relevant variables in our model have autocorrelations of at least the first order. Therefore, a time series transfer function model is constructed next to identify and isolate the autocorrelations in the variables. These results are reported in Table 6.6. A correlogram of *RCSR$_t$* suggests a four-period seasonal difference.[5]

Table 6.6
Transfer Function Model Estimates of Real Common Stock Returns on Measures of Real Activity, 1947–82

	(t–Statistics in brackets)		
	Dependent Variable : RCSR$_t$		
	Error model		
	Four Period Seasonal Difference Process		White-noise Process
	(1)	(2)	(3)
Intercept	0.105	0.09	2.39
	(0.82)	(0.77)	(3.24)
RGNPt+1	5.2E-03	5.1E-03	6.5E-03
	(3.05)	(3.79)	(6.70)
-B1RGNPt+1	0.94	0.94	0.93
	(5.04)	(6.14)	(14.55)
TFPYt+2	-2.4E-02	-2.2E-02	-1.3E-02
	(-1.28)	(-1.86)	(-1.96)
-B1TFPYt+2	1.2E-02		
	(0.01)		
MRSt,t+1	-2.22	-2.51	-1.73
	(-2.17)	(-2.81)	(-2.97)
-B1MRSt,t+1	-0.25		
	(-0.54)		

Prewhitening factors for the input variables (transfer functions) were obtained from their respective correlograms. In Table 6.6 we also present the results of the transfer function model assuming a white noise error process. Given below is the transfer function model:

$$i(B)RCSR_t = \alpha + \beta m_1(B)RGNP_{t+1} + \gamma m_2(B)TFPY_{t+2} + \eta m_3(B)MRS_{t,t+1} + \epsilon_t$$

(5)

where

B = Backshift Operator

$i(B)$ $= (1 - B^4)$

$m_k(B) = (1 - kB^1)$

ϵ_t = White noise error
and all other variables are as defined before.

All the coefficients have the expected signs. Moreover, only the first-order difference of *RGNP* is significant; that of the *TFPY* and the *MRS* are not significant. Thus, prewhitening or filtering the explanatory time series to obtain residual white noise series only emphasizes the robustness of the results presented earlier.

Summary

Real common stock returns seem to impound information regarding the future state of the economy. While the market adopts a short-term view (one year into the future) to incorporate information regarding the demand side of the economy, it looks farther ahead (at least two years) to assess the supply side of the economy. Intuitively, this is appealing. During the last three decades, government public policy had emphasized demand management. The stock market has thus come to expect frequent changes in the demand forces of the economy. Under these conditions, the appropriate time horizon over which expectations of the economy are to be formed is the short term. On the other hand, the neglect of supply-oriented policies during 1947 to 1982 (the period considered in our study) and the generally significant supply elasticities over longer time periods argue for the adoption of a longer term view to assess the supply side responses of the economy. Marginal rate of substitution between current and future consumption, representing the risk attitude (toward consumption) of the economy, is a significant determinant of market return. Significance tests of the multiperiod *MRS* indicate that the economy is more risk averse than risk neutral. This risk aversion in the aggregate has implications for the choice of discount rates and the rate of time preference utilized in public project evaluation. Finally, this study also points to the importance, for asset pricing, of the correlation of asset payoffs with aggregate consumption stream.

THE STOCK MARKET AND THE FIRM

In this section we seek to determine whether the stock market can successfully predict a firm's impending bankruptcy. While Chapter 5 considered the possibility of predicting reorganization pursuant to a bankruptcy, here we intend to harness the predictive power of the stock market to gauge the probability of bankruptcy of a failing but as yet nonbankrupt firm.

Financial Analysis and the Bankrupt Firm

Financial analysts and credit managers often attempt to predict the likelihood of financial difficulties by analyzing the financial aspects of the firm over a long period of time.[6] A popular method used in such analysis is the multiple discriminant analysis (MDA). The foremost proponent in the development and application of MDA to bankruptcy prediction is Edward Altman. Altman (1968) considered a sample of 66 manufacturing firms, half of which went bankrupt. He obtained 22 financial ratios, of which 5 were found to contribute most to the prediction model. The discriminant function Z was found to be

$$Z = .012X_1 + .014X_2 + .033X_3 + .006X_4 + .999X_5 \qquad (6)$$

where
X_1 = Working capital/Total assets (%)
X_2 = Retained earnings/Total assets (%)
X_3 = *EBIT*/Total assets (%)
X_4 = Equity (Market value)/Debt (Book value) (in %)
X_5 = Sales/Total assets (times)

The midpoint of the range of values of Z that results in minimal misclassifications was found to be 2.675. Thus, a firm with a Z score greater (less) than 2.675 is classified as a nonbankrupt (bankrupt) firm. The profitability ratio (X_3) was found to be the largest contributor to group separation. In a later study, Altman (1971) reported the group means for his groups of bankrupt and nonbankrupt firms:

	Bankrupt	Nonbankrupt	F Ratio
X_1	−6.1%	41.4%	32.60*
X_2	−62.6%	25.5%	58.86*
X_3	−31.8%	15.4%	26.56*
X_4	40.1%	247.7%	33.26*
X_5	150.0%	190.0%	2.84

(*Significant at the .001 level.)

It was found that the model correctly classified 72 percent of the sample two years prior to bankruptcy. Also, all the five observed ratios—X_1, . . . , X_5—deteriorated as bankruptcy approached and the most serious change in the majority of these ratios occurred between the third and second years prior to failure.

In contrast to the financial analysis described above, we will next consider a predictive framework based on the forecasting power of the stock market. How early can the stock market detect the impending financial bankruptcy of a firm in ill-health?

Stock Market Analysis and the Bankrupt Firm

The objectives of this analysis are to determine: (1) When does the stock market first perceive the impending bankruptcy of a potentially bankrupt firm? (2) What firm specific factors explain the duration between the perception time and the eventual date of bankruptcy (i.e.,

market lead time)?[7] Assuming market efficiency, the random walk stochastic generation process of the market return is expected to change its
parameters (mean and variance) on perception of impending bankruptcy
of the firm. The purpose of this analysis is to determine the time when
such a parametric change occurs in the return generation process. Also,
since market speed of adjustment to perception of bankruptcy will be a
function of the dependability of the signal perceived by the market (the
less dependable the signal, the longer the duration taken by the market
to adjust to the information regarding potential bankruptcy), we seek to
identify the firm-specific factors that convey to the market the dependability of the perceived bankruptcy signal.

Two distinct strands of research are identifiable in the area of bankruptcy prediction. One set of studies (Beaver, 1968a, 1968b; Altman,
1968, 1971; Altman, Haldeman, and Narayanan, 1977) tries to identify
key firm-specific ratios whose values when tracked provide an early
warning signal of impending failure. (Please see the previous section on
"Financial Analysis and the Bankrupt Firm" for a description of this
methodology.) These studies (with the exception of Beaver, 1968b), do
not focus on stock market reaction to potential bankruptcy. The other
set of studies (Aharony et al., 1980; Altman and Brenner, 1981; Clark
and Weinstein, 1983) investigates the behavior of abnormal market returns of potentially bankrupt companies. These event studies, while being
unable to refute market efficiency, find persistence of negative abnormal
market returns for one to three years. These studies do not distinguish
between any two potentially bankrupt firms in terms of stock market
reaction to their impending bankruptcy. The averaging technique employed in these event studies implies that the speed of adjustment of
market return to bankruptcy information is identical across firms.

The current analysis clearly demonstrates the bias that results from
the imposition of a single, arbitrary event period on every firm in a market efficiency study. (Brown, Lockwood and Lummer [1985] formally
demonstrate this bias and conclude by citing Bar-Yosef and Brown's
[1977] reexamination of the Fama et al. [1969] study that event periods
are more appropriately considered on a firm-by-firm basis.) Our analysis
also suggests that the firm-specific characteristics may cause differences in the stock market lead time in perceiving potential bankruptcies.

The time when the stock market first perceives the impending bankruptcy of the firm is defined as the stock market *perception time*. We
begin by determining the stock market perception time individually for
each potentially bankrupt firm. Hillmer and Yu (1979) suggested a statistical method to measure the time it takes security market attributes to
reflect new information. This method is used to measure the market perception time of bankrupt firms. The duration between the perception

time and the date of bankruptcy, defined here as the market *lead time*, is then explained in terms of firm-specific factors.

Model

Let us assume that the stock price changes are lognormally distributed. (This accounts for the limited liability of a stockholder in an efficient market.) Thus, the stock* price dynamics, in discrete time, are represented by

$$\text{Log } \frac{S_t}{S_{t-1}} = X_t$$
$$= \mu + \epsilon_t \tag{7}$$

where
S_t = Stock price at time t
μ = mean of log return
$\epsilon_t \cong N(0, \sigma^2)$

Under the efficient market hypothesis, values of μ and σ^2 impound all the information pertinent to the firm available at time t. Under this hypothesis, parameters μ and σ^2 change only when new information becomes available. The problem then is to determine if the parameters μ and σ^2 changed and, if so, when. These changes are assumed to be due to the information regarding impending bankruptcy of the firm. (Obviously, the parameter changes could reflect information about any number of firm-relevant events. However, it is reasonable to assume that the bankruptcy information swamps the effect of other events as the bankruptcy date approaches.)

Briefly, if $\{X_t | t = 0,1,2, \ldots, t_2\}$ is a stochastic process of market returns of a firm beginning with some start date $t=0$, t_2, the bankruptcy date, and t_1, the time at which a structural shift occurs in the mean return, then we have

$$\begin{aligned} X_t &= \mu + \epsilon_t, & t &= 0,1,2, \ldots, t_1 \text{ and,} \\ &= \mu_c + \epsilon_t, & t &= t_1 + 1, \ldots, t_2 \end{aligned} \tag{8}$$

where
t_1 = the time when market first perceives the future state of bankruptcy (this is
    indicated by a change in the parameter μ to μ_c)
t_2 = date of bankruptcy

The problem is to determine the time t_1 given the change in the parameter μ. If the structural shift is in the variance of market returns (σ^2) then we need to determine t_1^* such that

$$X_t = \mu + \epsilon_t, \qquad\qquad t = 0,1,2, \ldots, t_1^*$$
$$= \mu_c + \epsilon_t^*, \qquad\qquad t = t_1^* + 1, \ldots, t_2 \qquad (9)$$

where

$$\epsilon_t \cong N(O, \sigma^2)$$
$$\epsilon_t^* \cong N(O, \sigma_c^2)$$

The procedure to detect the structural change in the parameters is based upon the cumulative sum tests. Given the random process of $\{X\}$, the sum of the deviations of X from its parameter μ can be expected to be a symmetric Weiner process; subsequent to the structural change in the parameter the sum will be expected to possess a drift. Specifically, let

$$S_k = \sum_{t=t_s}^{k} (X_t - \theta) = \sum_{t=t_s}^{k} Y_t,$$

$$\qquad (10)$$

where Y_t is the deviation from the parameter θ. Intuitively, the cumulative sum S_k will move away from zero if the parameter changes from θ to θ_c. To incorporate this statistically, for every period k, a constant δ_k is constructed such that

Prob. $(S_j \leq \delta_j$ for some $j \leq k |$No parameter change$) = \alpha$

Then a change in the parameter is signaled whenever $S_k \leq \delta_k$. Thus, the probability of signaling a change in the parameter on or before time k, if in fact there was no change, is equal to α. Assuming the symmetric Weiner process for S_t it can be easily shown that

$$\delta_k = -\sqrt{k\tau} Z_{\alpha/2} \qquad (11)$$

where $Z_{\alpha/2}$ is such that $N(Z_{\alpha/2}) = 1 - \alpha/2$, $N(x)$ is the cumulative distribution function of the standard normal distribution and α is the level of confidence. Figure 6.1 depicts the different sequence of events at different points in time.

Stock market perception time, t_1, is then computed as follows (please refer to Hillmer and Yu, 1979):

$$t_1 = T - \frac{\delta_\tau}{\theta_c - \theta} \qquad (12)$$

where
T = time when statistically significant change in the parameter is signaled
δ_t = critical value estimated for a given level of confidence
θ = parameter (mean or variance of return) value before the change
θ_c = parameter value after the change

Figure 6.1
Time Sequence of Events

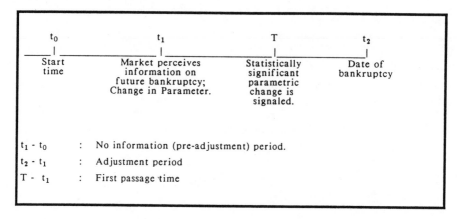

Stock market lead time is the duration from the market perception time t_1 to the date of bankruptcy, t_2. Thus,

$$\text{Stock market lead time} = t_2 - t_1 \tag{13}$$

Given below is an illustration of the Hillmer-Yu procedure applied to a bankrupt firm—Itel Corporation.

Illustration of a Change in Mean Return: Itel Corporation. Itel Corporation filed for bankruptcy on January 21, 1981. It was later reorganized and survived as a firm. This illustration determines the stock market perception time of Itel's impending bankruptcy of 1981.

Computational steps involve estimating the mean and variance of monthly total stock return during the preadjustment period and the adjustment period. The longer term nature of the bankruptcy event is likely to be discerned by monthly returns rather than the more volatile daily returns, which are subject to the impact of day-to-day events. Hillmer and Yu (1979, pp. 338–39) developed analytical bounds for the probability of detecting a parameter change and concluded that the chance of detecting a change increases as the length of the adjustment period, $t_2 - t_1$, increases. The market perception time, t_1, in equation 12 will be larger for daily returns as $\theta_c - \theta$ is larger for daily relative to monthly returns. Hence, the monthly returns will be more appropriate than the daily returns for the purpose of our analysis.

As shown in Figure 6.1, the adjustment period starts close to the perception time t_1 and continues until the date of bankruptcy, t_2. These periods are initially determined through a visual inspection of the graph of total stock return of the firm. The adjustment-free period usually ends a few months prior to the start of the adjustment period. Critical values,

Table 6.7
Itel Corporation: Market Perception Time and Mean Return

Pre-adjustment period	: May 1976—March 1978
Mean monthly total return during pre-adjustment period	: 0.026549
Adjustment period	: December 1978—January 1981
Mean monthly total return during adjustment period	: -0.09365
Structural change in mean signaled at T	: May 1979
Adjustment start time t_1	: January 1979
Date of Bankruptcy	: January 21, 1981
Stock market perception time (lead time)	: 24 months

δ_k's, (at 5% level of significance), and adjustment start time, t_1, are then computed for this initial adjustment period. The final adjustment period is obtained iteratively. The iteration is stopped when t_1 for two successive iterations is not significantly different.

Market perception time t_1^* can also be computed for a change in the parameter σ^2. Although the mean μ normally is expected to decrease on receipt of future bankruptcy information, the variance parameter σ^2 could increase due to increased uncertainty of the future. The same sequence of steps described earlier is undertaken to compute t_1^*. Table 6.7 contains the information on mean monthly returns for Itel Corporation while Figure 6.2 illustrates graphically the behavior of critical values, δ_k's, and the cumulative sum of deviations from the mean return during the adjustment period.

Illustration of a Change in Variance of Return: Itel Corporation. Market perception time, t_1^*, can also be computed for a change in the parameter σ^2. While the mean μ normally decreases on receipt of information regarding future bankruptcy, the variance parameter σ^2 could be expected to increase due to increased uncertainty of the future. The same sequence of steps described earlier is undertaken to compute t_1^*. Table 6.8 and Figure 6.3 illustrate the computation of t_1^* for a change in the variance parameter for Itel Corporation.

Figure 6.2
Itel Corporation: Mean Returns and Critical Values

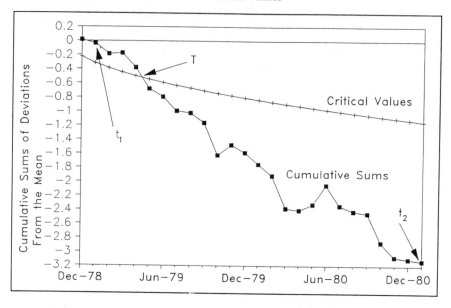

Table 6.8
Itel Corporation: Market Perception Time and Variance of Return

Pre-adjustment period	: May 1976—March 1978
Return variance during pre-adjustment period	: 0.0124488
Adjustment period	: December 1978—January 1981
Return variance during adjustment period	: 0.044037
Structural change in variance signaled at T	: May 1979
Adjustment start time t_1^*	: March 1979
Date of Bankruptcy	: January 21, 1981
Stock market perception time (lead time)	: 22 months

Figure 6.3
Itel Corporation: Return Variances and Critical Values

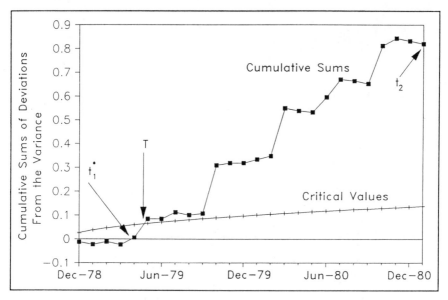

Lead Times and Explanatory Variables

As argued at the beginning of this section, market lead time, $t_2 - t_1$, need not be the same for any two companies nor for the two parameters μ and σ^2. However, most previous studies implicitly assumed that the stock market reacts with the same lead time for all the potentially bankrupt firms. At the least, there is an assumption of identical behavior (distributional parameters) of market returns across firms during the adjustment period. We found this not to be the case. Market perception times computed for a sample of 47 industrial firms yielded a range of values (see Table 6.9). We are therefore compelled to investigate further the differential perception of the market toward potentially bankrupt firms. What firm-specific characteristics could possibly explain this difference in perception times?

Altman's (1968) study of bankrupt firms indicates the importance of total assets while Basu's (1983) study points to some earnings measure as indicators of a firm's health. Aharony et al. (1980) tested the significance of systematic risk, β, as a useful indicator of firm deterioration over time. These variables are therefore tested as explanatory variables of lead times for the mean and variance of stock market returns of potentially bankrupt firms. Hence, it is hypothesized that

$$(t_2 - t_1)_i = f(A, B, \beta) \tag{14}$$

Table 6.9
Stock Market Perception Time for Mean Return and Variance of Return

Firms	Lead Time (Months)	
	Mean	Variance
1 AM International	13	20
2 Allied Stores	55	53
3 Ancorp	45	61
4 Apco Oil	12	15
5 Apeco	44	50
6 Arctic	18	30
7 Bobbie Brooks	60	59
8 Braniff	22	3
9 Chicago Milwau	28	28
10 Chicago Rock	81	10
11 City Stores	47	46
12 Colonial Comm.	32	30
13 Combustion	11	10
14 Comm. Oil	25	24
15 Continental	10	42
16 Daylin	9	11
17 Duplan/ Panex	5	9
18 Food Fair	14	17
19 Goldblatt	1	7
20 Grant - WT	27	24
21 Gray	11	25
22 Hajoca Corp.	29	22
23 Interstate	14	13
24 Itel Corp.	24	22

for $i = 1$, lead time for a change in μ

$\quad = 2$, lead time for a change in σ^2

where

$A \quad =$ Asset size of the firm at time t_1

$B \quad =$ Earnings per share of the firm at time t_1

$\beta \quad =$ Systematic risk of the firm during the pre-adjustment period

In an efficient market new information is conveyed by changes in the variables (innovations) rather than by their levels. Thus changes in lead times ought to be explained by changes in the explanatory variables of equation 14. It is as if, once the market perceives an impending bankruptcy, the probability of its immediacy changes based on new information (signals) received at the time of the initial perception. Thus, the time left to file for bankruptcy (lead time) changes based on new information received at time t_1. We test the following hypothesis:

Table 6.9 (continued)

Firms	Lead Time (Months)	
	Mean	Variance
25 KDT	28	11
26 Manville	17	30
27 Mays JW Inc.	40	31
28 Mc Louth	30	35
29 Morse Shoe	51	52
30 Neisner	21	14
31 Penn Dixie	7	10
32 Penn Fruit	48	22
33 RPS Products	10	6
34 Republic Brass	15	17
35 Richton Internl.	18	7
36 Sambos	6	4
37 Saxon	19	3
38 Seatrain	6	4
39 Shelter Resources	15	3
40 Telecor	17	16
41 UNR Industries	15	11
42 United Merchants	5	9
43 West Chemical	7	4
44 Whippany Paper	3	4
45 White Cross	40	36
46 Wickes	9	3
47 Winston Mills	10	6

$$Log\ (t_2 - t_1)_i = g(\phi, \psi) \tag{15}$$

for $i = 1$, lead time for a change in μ

$\quad\quad = 2$, lead time for a change in σ^2

where

$\phi\quad$ = rate of growth of assets at time t_1

$\psi\quad$ = rate of growth of earnings per share at time t_1

Data

A list of bankrupt firms was developed from *The Wall Street Journal Index*. Date of bankruptcy for each firm was identified from *Wall Street Journal* articles referencing these firms. Stock market return information was obtained from CRSP and the relevant COMPUSTAT tapes. These were supplemented by data from Moody's manuals. A list of 47 bankrupt industrial firms was then developed for which stock market monthly returns for at least five to six years prior to bankruptcy could be ob-

Table 6.10
Frequency Distribution of Lead Times

Class Interval (Months)	Mean Return		Variance of Return	
	Observed frequency	Cumulative percentage	Observed frequency	Cumulative percentage
Less than 9	10	21.3	14	29.8
9 - 18	16	55.3	12	55.3
18 - 27	6	68.1	7	70.2
27 - 36	5	78.7	7	85.1
36 - 45	4	87.2	1	87.2
45 - 54	3	93.6	4	95.7
54 - 63	2	97.9	2	100.0
63 - 72	0	97.9	0	100.0
72 - 81	1	100.0	0	100.0
TOTAL	47		47	

Note: Computed Chi-square is 38.596 and 31.128 for mean and variance of return respectively. Thus the null hypothesis of uniform distribution is rejected for both the lead times at 1% level of significance and their respective degrees of freedom.

tained. Systematic risk of these firms was computed with reference to a market index based on all firms listed on the New York and American Stock Exchanges. Data on assets and earnings per share (EPS) of the firms were obtained from COMPUSTAT, Value-Line, and Moody's manuals.

Results and Analysis

Stock market lead times for the mean and variance of monthly total stock returns are computed for a sample of 47 bankrupt industrial firms. The lead times are given in Table 6.9. A goodness-of-fit Chi-square test performed under the null hypothesis of uniform distribution of the lead times is rejected. Results of the test are given in Table 6.10. Clearly, not all possible lead times are equally likely. A little more than 50% of the firms have lead times of less than 18 months.

As hypothesized in equation 15, market lead times for the mean, *LEADMEAN,* and the variance of return, *LEADVAR,* are regressed separately against the asset size of the firm, *ASTVAL,* earnings per share, *EPSVAL,* and the systematic risk, *BETANYAM,* of the firm. Systematic risk of the firm is computed for the pre-adjustment period $(t_1 - t_0)$, while asset size and EPS are computed for time t_1, the market perception time. Various asset and EPS measures are also computed for time t_1, the market perception time of bankruptcy. Thus the regression equations tested are:

$$LEADMEAN_j = a_1 + b_1 BETANYAM_j + c_1 ASTVALMN_j$$
$$+ d_1 EPSVALMN_j + \epsilon_{1j} \tag{16}$$

$$LEADVAR_j = a_2 + b_2 BETANYAM_j + c_2 ASTVALVA_j$$
$$+ d_2 EPSVALVA_j + \epsilon_{2j} \tag{17}$$

where $j = 1, 2, 3, \ldots 47$; (number of firms)

Results of the cross-sectional regressions 16 and 17 are given in Table 6.11 as equations 1 and 4. Low values of R^2 are attributable to the cross-sectional nature of the data. For both the lead times, neither the systematic risk nor the asset size of the firm is significant. In this, the result supports the finding of Aharony et al. (1980) that systematic risk, β, is not a useful indicator of firm deterioration over time. Effects of EPS on lead times is both positive and significant. The stock market places a higher probability of survival (hence, a longer lead time) on the potentially bankrupt firm with a higher EPS at the time of market perception of future bankruptcy.

As was explained earlier, the effect of new information on market lead times is assessed through the following regression equations:

$$Log(LEADMEAN)_j = LLDMN_j = a_3 + b_3 ASTCHGMN_j$$
$$+ c_3 EPSCHGMN_j + \epsilon_{3j} \tag{18}$$

$$Log(LEADVAR)_j = LLDVA_j = a_4 + b_4 ASTCHGVA_j + c_4 EPSCHGVA_j$$
$$+ \epsilon_{4j} \tag{19}$$

where $j = 1, 2, 3, \ldots 47$; (number of firms)
and where *ASTCHG* and *EPSCHG* are percentage changes in total assets and EPS respectively, at time t_1. These percentage changes are computed separately at the corresponding market perception time for the mean and variance of return.

Results of the regressions 18 and 19 are given in Table 6.11, as equations 2 and 5. Again, small values of R^2 are indicative of the cross-sectional nature of the data used. Only the asset change variable is positively and significantly related to the percentage change in lead times. Between two similar firms that have been signaled by the market as potentially bankrupt, the one with the higher level of investment is likely to have a longer market lead time. Presumably, investment commitments by the potentially bankrupt firm at time t_1 convey information enabling assessment of probability of survival. Finally, as equation 3 of Table 6.11 indicates, EPS is significantly and positively related to percentage change in lead time for mean market return. In the case of EPS, it is the level rather than the change that seems to convey information to the security market.

The variance of return increases structurally, at time t_1, in 46 out of

Investing in Financially Distressed Firms

Table 6.11
Lead Time and Firm-Specific Explanatory Variables

Dependent Variable	Explanatory Variables						R^2
	CON-STANT	BETA-NYAM	AST-VAL	EPS-VAL	AST-CHG	EPS-CHG	
Mean of Stock Return							
1. LEADMEAN	28.3	-2.76	-0.007	0.634			0.12
	(4.43)	(-.124)	(-1.51)	(1.83)			
2. LLDMN	2.63				1.38	-0.014	0.15
	(19.9)				(2.59)	(-1.04)	
3. LLDMN	2.72			0.043	0.983		0.24
	(22.3)			(2.48)	(1.88)		
Variance of Stock Return							
4. LEADVAR	29.9	-4.22	-0.007	0.726			0.15
	(4.44)	(-0.911)	(-1.31)	(2.27)			
5. LLDVA	2.65				1.51	0.005	0.14
	(19.4)				(2.5)	(0.62)	
6. LLDVA	2.67			0.026	1.08		0.17
	(20.1)			(1.43)	(1.64)		

Note: Please refer to the text for an explanation of the variables. The numbers in the parentheses are t-statistics.

the 47 firms, whereas the mean parameter increases in 10 out of the 47 firms of the sample. While the increase in return variance in the face of an impending bankruptcy is understandable, the increase in the ex-post mean return is intriguing. This might suggest the presence of two different types of investors—the speculator-investor and the "common" risk-averse investor—at time t_1 of a potentially bankrupt firm. The firm that succeeds in attracting the speculator might see an increase in its mean return despite market perception of impending bankruptcy. More research, of course, needs to be done to understand the roles of these two types of investors at play in the market. What factors cause some potentially bankrupt firms to attract more of one or the other type of investor could prove to be an intriguing subject for future research.

SUMMARY

While there exists significant literature in the area of bankruptcy prediction utilizing accounting data of the firm, using stock market data to perform the same has been rather limited. Given the general acceptance of the notion of the market being able to price securities efficiently this is rather surprising. We present a method that uses the market's capability to incorporate information about potential financial distress of a firm.

Market efficiency studies concerning effect of major events on a firm's stock price have generally assumed a single arbitrary event period. Such an assumption is questionable. In the case of a sample of potentially bankrupt firms this assumption implies uniform behavior of stock market returns across firms prior to bankruptcy. The current study's findings warrant caution on that assumption.

A computational methodology based on the Hillmer-Yu technique is suggested to measure the time when a parametric change occurs in the market return mean and variance of a potentially bankrupt firm. This parametric change time is defined as the time when the stock market first perceives the eventual bankruptcy of the firm. The lead time interval or the duration from market perception time to the date of eventual bankruptcy is determined for a sample of 47 bankrupt industrial firms.

The lead time interval (for both the mean and variance of monthly market return) of potentially bankrupt firms is found to be positively and significantly related to the firm's EPS at the time of stock market perception of eventual bankruptcy. Neither the firm's asset size nor systematic risk appear to be significant indicators of lead time interval. Change in investment (change in total assets) by the firm at time t_1 is positively related to percentage change in market lead time. This suggests that innovation in the investment variable are a source of new information to the security market in reassessing the probability of future bankruptcy of a firm. The fact that in some cases mean returns increased at time t_1 through date of bankruptcy indicates the need for more research to determine the factors that might attract different types of investors to a potentially bankrupt firm.

NOTES

1. For an excellent review of the theory and evidence of efficient capital markets, see Copeland and Weston (1983).

2. Breeden (1979) gives a numerical example on p. 279 to illustrate the main point of his paper. In that example he uses physical productivity as a proxy for investment opportunity in a given state.

3. Consider a consumer with a utility function:

$$^{a}U_t = \sum_{k=0}^{\infty} \beta^k u(C_{t+k}),$$

where $\beta = 1/(1+r)$ and r is the subjective rate of time preference. Given that the consumer maximizes the expectation at time t of this utility function, a necessary condition for optimal holding of the asset at time t is:

$u'(C_t)P_t = \beta E(u'[c_{t+1}][P_{t+1} + D_{t+1}]$ where P_t and D_t are the real price and dividend of the asset. If $MRS_{t,t+1} = \beta u'(C_{t+1})/u'(C_t)$ is the marginal rate of substitution between present and future consumption then, equation 3 follows.

4. $MRS_{t,t+2}$ was also found to be significant in most cases. Coefficient for *MRS* between consumption of periods separated by more than two years were found to be insignificant.

5. Fama (1981) also obtains a near-significant fourth-order autocorrelation for the real stock return (compare his Table 4, p. 554). The implication of this is as yet unclear unless it has something to do with the quadrennial presidential elections.

6. This section draws from Altman (1968) and Appendix B to Chapter 8 of Weston and Copeland (1986).

7. This section draws heavily from Ramaswami (1987).

Case Studies

MCORP

In October 1988 the management of MCorp faced a painful decision. Continuing loan losses had forced them to ask the Federal Deposit Insurance Corporation (FDIC) for aid. Management hoped for a restructuring of MCorp's assets, which would allow the company to continue functioning as a bank holding company. In the interim MCorp had stopped all dividend and interest payments on its securities. At the time MCorp had not filed for Chapter 11 protection of its assets, but if it did file, experts estimated it would take three to five years before a reorganization plan would be in place.

Heinrich Maxim, head of a New York-based investment firm that speculates in the securities of financially distressed firms, asked his staff to review the financial and legal position of MCorp. He wanted a recommendation on whether the firm should buy any of MCorp's securities. If such a recommendation was made he needed to known which securities should be purchased and at what price and when the purchase should be made.

Background

MCorp, one of the largest commercial banks in Texas, was formed on October 10, 1984, by the merger of Mercantile Texas Corporation and Southwest Bancshares, Inc.[1] A major part of MCorp's lending activities historically has been to the energy and real estate industries in the Southwest. As a result of the collapse in oil prices and excessive over-building in the real estate sector, MCorp, along with virtually all of its regional competitors, experienced substantial asset quality problems be-ginning in the mid-1980s. The severity of these problems was made clear when MCorp announced provisions for loan losses of $258 million in 1987 and $551 million in the first nine months of 1988. MCorp's banking units posted a total loss of $903 million for 1988, according to a prelimi-nary report filed with the FDIC. In 1987 the banking units reported a total loss of $174 million. At the end of 1988, MCorp banks reported total deposits of $14.8 billion, down sharply from $17.2 billion at the end of 1987.[2] Non-performing assets increased from $1.2 billion at the end of 1986 to $2.0 billion on September 30, 1988.

The continued erosion in asset quality forced MCorp to improve its primary and total capital by selling assets and raising additional capital. In 1985 MCorp placed $350 million in new preferred stock and subordi-nated debentures. In 1986 the company sold its MNet subsidiary for $300 million and sold 20% of MTech, MCorp's data processing operations, for $38 million in a public offering. MCorp sold the remaining 80% of MTech to EDS for $281 million in early 1988. In spite of these measures, continuing loan losses led MCorp to seek assistance from the FDIC in October 1988.

MCorp's proposal to the FDIC included the downstreaming of $400 million of assets to its bank subsidiaries, the infusion of $400 million of new equity capital, and a loan from the government of $1 billion. The FDIC initially refused to consider any proposal prior to MCorp's down-streaming assets to the troubled subsidiary banks. At the same time, the Board of Governors of the Federal Reserve Board issued a temporary order directing MCorp not to declare dividends on its equity securities or otherwise dissipate the assets of the Parent. MCorp responded by suspending payments on all Parent securities, including its publicly held bonds. On November 6, 1988, MCorp and the FDIC reached an agree-ment whereby the FDIC and the Comptroller of the Currency agreed to suspend actions against MCorp while the FDIC considered recapitaliza-tion proposals by the Company and other outside parties. MCorp, for its part, agreed to allow free access to its books and records to potential third-party investors.

On October 21, 1988, MCorp failed to pay interest when due on its floating rate notes maturing in 1992. These bonds went into default when the 30-day grace period ended in November. Under the cross default provisions of the remaining Parent bonds, all Parent debentures are now in default. Consequently, any three bondholders may file an involuntary bankruptcy petition against MCorp. Bondholders may also accelerate the maturity of any of the individual instruments with the approval of 25%

of each issue. Bondholders have not taken actions to date to force a bankruptcy and are unlikely to do so prior to MCorp proposing an exchange offer or the FDIC initiating actions to downstream assets without bondholders' consent.

Financial Analysis

Table 7.1 lists all of the securities held by MCorp in October 1988. The company's balance sheet is shown on Table 7.2. The balance sheet was prepared by MCorp's management and distributed at a creditors' meeting.

Analysis of the balance sheet indicates that if the company is forced to liquidate, senior debtholders can receive 100% of their capital. MCorp's assets are principally cash and marketable securities and thus very liquid with a ready market. The value of their claim is $343 million while total assets are listed at $369.7 million. The difference between $369.7 million and $343 million of $26.7 million would be distributed among subordinated debtholders. They would receive 21 cents on each dollar invested.

If Maxim bought the senior debt at its current price of $43 and bankruptcy occurred, he would receive all of his investment back less interest if the company was liquidated, since the bonds are in default. It appears to be a risk-free investment as far as the capital is concerned. Buying the subordinated bonds at $27 represents more risk for Maxim if MCorp files for bankruptcy, but the upside potential of the subordinated bonds is high if the firm is able to restructure its assets. The most risky investment is the firm's equity. However, as the equity was selling at 50 cents a share, any restructuring plan should help increase investor confidence in the stock. If the price rises to $1.00 per share, an investor would have earned a handsome 100% return.

Restructuring Plan

MCorp has proposed a bailout plan through which $400 million of Parent assets and $400 million of new equity would be contributed to the insolvent subsidiary banks on the condition the FDIC lends those subsidiaries $1 billion. If the FDIC forces MCorp to file for bankruptcy, the courts may decide that the regulators are not entitled to Parent assets. A decision may take three years or more if the issue is litigated. Even if the FDIC eventually gets access to the Parent assets, the present value of those assets may be considerably less than the current market value. A bankruptcy may instigate a run on the deposits of the subsidiaries, further increasing the cost of a bailout. The costs of administering the Chapter 11 will reduce the value of the estate as well.

In the event that the FDIC decides to accept a restructuring proposal

Table 7.1
MCORP: Securities Description

Offer Year	Issue	Price[1]	Amount Outstanding (millions)
	SENIOR DEBT SECURITIES[2]		
1985	Floating Rate Notes of 7/17/92	$43.00	$100.00
1985	Medium-Term Notes, Series A	43.00	34.00
1983	10 5/8% Notes of 3/01/93	43.00	25.00
1982	11 1/2% Notes of 12/15/89	43.00	50.00
1982	11 1/2% of 11/15/92	43.00	50.00
1979	Floating Rate Notes of 7/15/99	43.00	35.00
1976	9 3/8% of 7/01/01	43.00	29.00
	SUBORDINATE DEBT SECURITIES		
1985	Subordinate Floating Rate Notes of 11/14/97	27.50	125.00
	EQUITY SECURITIES		
1982	$3.50 Cumulative Convertible Preferred[3]	5.25	0.960
	Series A Money Market Preferred[4]	Private	0.125
	Series B Money Market Preferred	Private	0.125
	Common Stock	0.50	42.45

Notes: 1.   Closing price as of 12/15/88
         2.   All senior unsecured issues are of equal rank in a bankruptcy. No MCorp bonds have original issue discounts.
         3. $50 liquidation preference
         4. $500,000 liquidation preference. Ranks senior to the $3.50 preferred with regard to proceeds from liquidation.

Source: R.D. Smith & Company report.

from another banking institution, the resultant management disruption could damage the business and increase the cost of a bailout. MCorp senior executives are generally well respected in the industry. They have performed well in light of the severity of the economic downturn in Texas. New management would almost certainly come from an out-of-state institution less familiar with the local market.

The type of restructuring plan MCorp would probably offer its securityholders would give senior bondholders new securities worth $60, a 40% premium to current prices. Payouts to the subordinated bondholders are less certain but would probably reach $40, a 45% premium to current prices.

Table 7.2
MCORP: Parent Company Balance Sheet Values (Millions)

ASSETS[1]		LIABILITIES	
Cash	$5.1	Senior Debt	$343.0
U.S. Government Securities	8.4	Subordinate Debt	125.0
Marketable Securities		Accrued Interest	22.4
General Motors[2]	141.9		
Lomas & Nettleton[3]	68.8	Total Liabilities	$490.4
Non-Marketable Securities	28.3		
Intercompany Loans:			
MVest	77.0		
Other Non-Bank Loans	2.7		
Commercial Loans	12.8		
Other	11.7		
Partnership Investments	13.0		
Total Assets per MCorp	$369.7		

Notes: 1. Fair market value of assets net of the equity in subsidiary banks as prepared by MCorp management.

2. Includes 3.1 million shares of General Motors Class E Stock with a $58 put
option exercisable in April 1991. The GME stock, currently trading at $42
per share, would be valued at $130 million and the put feature is valued by
management at $14 million.

3. The Lomas & Nettelton position consists of the following restricted securities:

Million		Price	Value
$35.50	8% Senior Notes due 12/31/93	$90.0	$32.0 mm
0.36	Preferred Stock $5 Dividend	51.0	18.4 mm
1.44	Common Stock	13.0	18.4 mm

Source: R.D. Smith & Company report.

Risks

The primary risks of investing in MCorp bonds are that the federal
bank regulators will require management to downstream MCorp parent
company assets to insolvent subsidiary banks without fair compensation, or that the government succeeds in creating claims against the estate of the Parent in bankruptcy sufficient to impair the asset coverage
of the bondholders. It could take three to five years to resolve these
questions in court if MCorp files for bankruptcy. Although MCorp has
strong legal arguments in support of retaining Parent assets for the benefit of creditors, a small chance of a complete loss of investment exists.

Investors should keep in mind that even if the regulators seize all Parent assets, the bonds should trade at substantially more than zero.

As long as MCorp stays out of bankruptcy, creditors must rely on management to negotiate an agreement acceptable to their interests. Management theoretically could strike a deal through which they were absolved from liability and retained their jobs at the expense of bondholders. The regulators could issue cease and desist orders prior to creditors filing an involuntary bankruptcy petition, potentially enhancing the regulators' position in the bankruptcy. Creditors will probably try to mitigate this risk by proposing a standstill agreement with the FDIC and management or by seeking other injunctive relief outside the bankruptcy court.

If MCorp files for bankruptcy the value of the estate could erode for several reasons, some of the most important of which include:

- Legal and other administrative costs of the bankruptcy should be substantial given the size and complexity of the case.
- MCorp runs the risk that a bankruptcy would lead to the immediate seizure of all subsidiary banks by the FDIC. In addition to losing any equity in the healthy subsidiaries, MCorp's trust operation, MTrust, could decline in value without the bank's ongoing business.

Conclusion

On March 16, 1989, a *Wall Street Journal* article reported that MCorp may experience larger loan losses than they at first anticipated. The banking units' reported 1988 loss of $903 million suggested that overall losses will be in the worst-case range of analysts' predictions. Many prospective bidders for the firm have been scared off. The rescue may require more than the $1 billion in federal assistance requested by MCorp management. Kohlberg Kravis Roberts & Company, the leveraged buyout specialist, remains interested, according to an inside source. Another group of potential investors—which includes Harry Gray, former United Technologies chairman; the Pritzker family of Chicago; and Dan Lufkin, a founder of the investment bank Donaldson, Lufkin & Jenrette Securities—was reported to be still interested in MCorp. Other bidders are reluctant to proceed until the issue of satisfying the holding company's creditors is first resolved. A few stubborn creditors might hold up any deal, as occurred in the FDIC's rescue in 1988 of First City Bancorp of Texas. MCorp's plan to restructure itself remains a possibility, although federal regulators have been loath to retain the management of rescued institutions.

Currently all debt instruments of MCorp are in default. MCorp shares traded at 46.875 cents at the close of March 15, 1989. Creditors could immediately accelerate the case and file an involuntary Chapter 11 petition. If bankruptcy occurs, an investor might find MCorp securities an attractive investment as many untested legal and regulatory issues have yet to be resolved in this case (see "Appendix").

Epilogue

MCorp's attempts to evade federal seizure of assets and also to stay out of bankruptcy court received a rude shock in March 1989 when three small MCorp creditors (one holding $2 million of MCorp debentures and the other two, $5,000 each) filed a court petition to have MCorp liquidated involuntarily under Chapter 7 of federal bankruptcy law. This set off a chain reaction resulting in the third largest banking failure in U.S. banking history. In response the Federal Reserve called its loan to MCorp's flagship bank, MBank Dallas, which, when it couldn't repay, dragged down most of the other MCorp banks. The FDIC consequently took control of 20 of MCorp's 25 banks with $15.4 billion in assets and $11.6 billion in deposits, leaving the holding company with five banks and $3 billion in assets. The FDIC had all along insisted that the holding company inject some $400 million into the troubled branches. With the federal takeover, the FDIC is planning to pursue "substantial" and "material" claims involving "transactions between the banks and the holding company."

MCorp management hit back with a flurry of legal maneuvers to block the federal takeover of its assets. The company filed a petition in bankruptcy court to convert the earlier petition by the three creditors seeking MCorp's liquidation under Chapter 7 into a request for protection under Chapter 11. Under federal bankruptcy law, MCorp's Chapter 11 filing supersedes the Chapter 7 petition. This bankruptcy filing by MCorp unsettles federal efforts to rescue MCorp by selling off the insolvent banks. The bankruptcy filing would put the holding company—along with some $400 million in assets and, possibly, whatever healthy banks MCorp owns—under the supervision of a bankruptcy judge. Thus, any federal plan to sell the whole package would be subject to the judge's approval. Some of the buyers could be scared away by the uncertainty involved in such a transaction. Thus, the smaller the proceeds from the asset sales due to the legal uncertainty associated with a bankruptcy filing, the more money the FDIC would have to lay out toward a rescue of MCorp banks. The company management also filed a suit against the regulators charging that the U.S. Comptroller of the Currency and the FDIC illegally seized the banks.

These suits have been filed to let MCorp be a serious bidder along with several large banks and financial concerns from whom the FDIC had solicited bids for the 20 banks that were taken over. The suits could also provide a forum to debate the extent to which the FDIC, in its efforts to keep the banking system healthy, can disregard and deny the rights of the creditors to be repaid.

Bond investors face an unusually tough call. Should they buy or hold the bonds of the beleaguered holding company, betting on its $250 million in liquid assets? Or stay away from the securities due to the legal and political risk associated with the major government claim on MCorp assets? The MCorp holding company appears to have a minimum of 80 cents and a maximum of 100 cents of assets behind every dollar of its senior credit. In recognition of this asset coverage MCorp's 1992 floating rate debenture (a bellwether issue for its senior debt), was trading on March 30, 1989, at 40 to 43 cents on the dollar, up from the prior week's low of 35 cents. Yet this is a case of known assets versus an unknowable risk associated with federal regulation.

Appendix: Legal Issues Affecting Creditors

According to the December 1988 report by R. D. Smith & Company, the best outcome for MCorp creditors would be if the company was reorganized. In the worst case, creditors and regulators will battle over their rights in bankruptcy court for years. The most important questions include:

1. What authority do the Federal Reserve Board and FDIC have to require MCorp to downstream Parent assets for the benefit of subsidiary banks?
2. In the event that MCorp files for bankruptcy, how is that authority reduced or enhanced? In particular, on what basis can regulators assert claims against a bankrupt holding company for the bailout of insolvent bank subsidiaries?
3. What authority does the Board and the FDIC have to merge subsidiary banks or force healthy subsidiaries into receivership?

In the case of MCorp the Parent holding company is not in financial trouble, but its bank subsidiaries are insolvent. The Federal Reserve's position is that the Parent should not withhold financial support from its subsidiaries—or it should downstream its assets to its financially distressed subsidiaries. The Federal Reserve views a bank holding company's failure to assist a troubled subsidiary bank as an unsafe and unsound banking practice. The real question is can they legally force MCorp to give aid to these subsidiaries. If MCorp files for Chapter 11 protection the government will probably attempt to enforce a cease and desist order requiring the downstreaming of parent assets. The crucial question is not whether the automatic stay applies or is vacated, however, but whether Chapter 11 will provide relief from the claims and fines levied by the regulators.

Another critical question in the MCorp case is whether the FDIC can compel solvent banks to merge with insolvent bank subsidiaries or seize solvent banks as a way to prevent Parent creditors from realizing value in the equity of those subsidiaries. Congress has yet to pass a bill that would require bank holding companies to act as a single bank, establishing the principle that the financial strength of the healthy segment of a holding company be used to save a subsidiary. The history of the First Republic Bank Corporation collapse further supports the contention that the regulators do not have clear authority to order reorganizations or mergers in a failing bank situation. In First Republic, the FDIC was able to seize the healthy subsidiary banks by rendering them insolvent through a complex lending arrangement. First Republic's Houston and Dallas branches were loaned $1 billion on the condition that those loans be guaranteed by all of the subsidiary banks. Once those loans were in place, the FDIC called them, creating an immediate insolvency at the healthy banks. The fact that the FDIC concocted such a scheme to render healthy banks insolvent suggests that it had no independent authority to seize or force the merger of the solvent subsidiaries. However, it does not mean that just because the FDIC does not have clear authority to seize healthy bank assets to help an insolvent bank, they can not do it anyway.

MANVILLE CORPORATION

Manville, a Denver-based construction and forest products company, filed for Chapter 11 protection of its assets on August 26, 1982. At the time, the company was the world's largest asbestos manufacturer. Manville's management filed for Chapter 11 under the 1978 Bankruptcy Reform Act after losing a major legal battle. The victims of asbestos-related diseases won a settlement of approximately $2 billion dollars against the company. This settlement was nearly twice the company's net worth of $1.1 billion.

Background

The plaintiffs in the lawsuit against Manville were government shipyard workers, pipe fitters, installation workers, Manville employees, and other persons who worked with products containing asbestos. They claimed that Manville should be liable for the diseases they contracted from working with asbestos, even though no one knew at the time of their exposure to asbestos that it was a health hazard.

Asbestos, a soft fiber that once was the most widely used insulation material in the United States, is blamed for two fatal diseases: asbestosis, which dramatically cuts breathing capacity; and mesothelioma, a cancer of the lung lining that suffocates the victim. As more people who worked with asbestos were afflicted with one of these diseases, scientists and attorneys gathered evidence that the fiber was responsible and began suing manufacturers.

During the late 1970s and early 1980s Manville and other asbestos producers and users were hit by medical claims from people who believed they had been injured by working with or around asbestos. Initially Manville had asked the federal government to assume a major share of the cost because many workers incurred cancer or asbestosis from exposure to asbestos during wartime service in shipyards. The government bought and sold asbestos fiber, it purchased machinery to give to asbestos manufacturers, it specified the products and controlled the workplace where most of the workers had been exposed. At the time of its filing, Manville had 16,500 asbestos lawsuits pending and expected an additional 32,000 cases to be filed. The advantage of a bankruptcy filing for Manville was that it prohibited any new lawsuits being filed against it.

Testing the New Provisions of Chapter 11

At the time Manville filed, it was unclear whether the Chapter 11 petition would be upheld in court. Manville was one of the healthiest companies ever to file for reorganization. Manville gambled that its petition would be upheld in court. This would give Manville the advantage of having the 16,500 asbestos lawsuits pending against it consolidated in a single court before a single judge. This procedure would allow for quicker resolution of the cases and would trim the overwhelming legal costs of defending cases on an individual basis.

While some attorneys at the time believed that Manville's reorganization move would greatly benefit it by resolving asbestos litigation, it did present a number of risks for the company. Among them were the possible loss of confidence of the investors, creditors, and consumers. In addition there was the threat that the value of the stock owned by shareholders would be devalued. Manville's common stock traded at $7.88 a share at the close of business August 25, 1982, the day before the company filed its petition for reorganization under Chapter 11. The stock was trading for $5.00 a share one week later.

Owners and managers of the corporation would be closely scrutinized by the bankruptcy court and creditors and would not be in control of their own destiny. An intangible cost of being dropped as one of the companies included in the Dow Jones 30 Industrial Average was another risk. There also was no guarantee Manville would be successful in its attempt to reorganize. The company could ultimately be sold off piece-by-piece to meet its obligations if it was forced into a Chapter 7 liquidation. To Manville's advantage, bankruptcy judges have enormous discretion and power when it comes to resolving claims against a company in reorganization.

Negative Net Worth from Settlement of Legal Claims

Why did Manville's management file for bankruptcy when they did? They had already paid some of the claims against it. One reason was that Manville's costs were mounting every day. Nearly one-fifth of what Manville spent on asbestos-injury cases was going to pay defense lawyers rather than victims. Manville had paid $57.6 million to dispose of claims and was appealing another $14.7 million worth of judgments in 23 pending verdicts. Manville estimated that the cost to dispose of a typical claim was about $40,000 a case. Under the contingent fee system, plaintiffs' lawyers often contract with clients to receive one-third of any claim, although the amount is negotiable. A one-third contingent fee would leave a typical claimant with $21,666 on a claim that cost Manville $40,000. As of June 30, 1982, Manville disposed of 698 claims during 1982 at an average cost, excluding defense legal fees and expenses, of $18,690 per claim. For all of 1981 and 1980, the comparable average claim cost was $15,025 and $22,710, respectively. The cumulative average claim disposal cost was $16,600 as of June 30, 1982, for the 3,470 claims resolved to date, excluding defense legal costs and verdicts in 23 cases that still needed to be reviewed or appealed. Simple multiplication revealed a cost of $57.6 million. If all 23 appeals were lost, the average disposal cost for 3,493 cases would rise to $20,690 per claim, which computes to a cost of $71.3 million. If this liability was added to the company's balance sheet then its assets would add to less than its liabilities. Therefore, the company's management believed that the settlements of the lawsuits would eventually bankrupt the company.

Reorganization Plan

At the time Manville filed for bankruptcy, it was given four months to devise a reorganization plan. Unfortunately it took six years for the company finally to emerge from Chapter 11 bankruptcy on November 28, 1988. By December 1982, more than 250 lawsuits had been filed against Manville officers and directors or its insurers. Manville was solvent when it filed in August 1982 and many people felt that the company was misusing the Bankruptcy Law in an effort to rid itself of pending lawsuits of asbestos victims. One of Manville's problems was that it did not have enough insurance to cover all the claims against it. By June 1984 it had finally received an offer from its three insurers to provide Manville with $315 million in coverage. Manville claimed it needed $600 million to complete a reorganization plan.

One of the first reorganization plans that Manville developed in June 1984 was one that intended to cover both present and future asbestos victims by calling for the creation of a $2 billion trust fund. The company would contribute $100 million in cash, the insurance companies would contribute $600 million, and an estimated $1.3 billion from 50 million shares of Manville common stock would also be added to the fund. Manville's operating businesses would be transferred to a new group of operating companies and would be protected from asbestos-related lawsuits by a permanent injunction issued by the bankruptcy court. Under the plan, a facility would be established to settle asbestos claims outside the court system while reserving a plaintiff's right to go to court if negotiations and arbitration failed. However, plaintiffs could no longer seek punitive damages from Manville. This plan was known as the Jamison plan after Dean John Jamison of the College of William and Mary, who framed it as a member of the Manville commercial creditors' committee. This plan was the basis for the final reorganization plan approved by the bankruptcy court. In the end all parties agreed to the plan except the company's equityholders, whose stock became very diluted.

The prime sticking point to consensus appeared to be Manville's insurers, which to a large extent forced the company into Chapter 11. After paying some early asbestos claims, the insurance companies began to challenge settlements more strenuously when punitive damages edged payments into the seven-digit range. In response, Manville sued its 27 insurers. A tentative settlement for $315 million was reached with three of its biggest insurers—Travelers, Home Insurance, and Lloyd's of London. By August 1984 it had yet to settle with another primary insurer, Commercial Union in Boston. Commercial Union felt confident at that time that it would beat Manville in court. Settling with the insurers was vital to the acceptance of the reorganization plan as Manville needed the insurance money to provide the initial funding for the trust.

Another obstacle to the acceptance of the plan was a mandatory vote by the shareholders. The plan would dilute their common stock by two-thirds if it went through. The key to whether any groups would accept the plan is their judgment as to the justice of the reorganization plan and the ability of the trust—which would be 50–60 percent funded by the stock of the operating company—to pay the claims against Manville.

Trust Funds for Asbestosis Sufferers

Manville created two trust funds to pay claimants of asbestosis sufferers. These funds are now worth $935 million. Through these trust funds the asbestosis victims now own 50% of the company. The company's profits (Manville no longer produces asbestos; it now makes fiberglass and processes forest products and is involved in mining and roofing) are expected to feed the fund and should meet the $3 billion of expected claims over the next 25 years.

Although Manville had originally maintained that the trust would be worth $2 billion, the immediate liquidation value of the trust in August

1984 was only $615 million, as the insurance companies had agreed to contribute only $315 million. Additionally, the common stock would have to quadruple in value from its $9 share price in August 1984 to meet the $2 billion target.

Manville and its claimants fine-tuned the above reorganization plan from August 1984 to the plan's final approval in December 1986. Manville finally emerged from bankruptcy only in November 1988 after the Supreme Court refused to hear the remaining appeal against the reorganization plan, which was filed by the MacArthur Company, a building-materials distributors based in Minneapolis. The appeal sought to reverse a ruling by a three-judge appellate panel in Manhattan by arguing that it was denied due process of law because the settlement bars vendors from asserting future claims against insurers. The final settlement was for a $3 billion trust. The insurance companies finally agreed to give about $770 million. Manville itself put up $815 million in cash and receivables. The trust also would receive $75 million per year from Manville for 24 years beginning three years after the trust's inception. The trust also would own or have access to up to 80 percent of Manville's common stock and the right to 20 percent of the corporation's profits beginning four years after its inception and continuing as long as necessary to pay asbestos injury claims.

One of the problems that Manville had faced during the years 1984 to 1986 was that the plaintiff's lawyers were to receive one-third of the trust's money for their services. Manville's creditors and shareholders at the same time believed that they were not being fairly treated. They wanted the lawyers to get less and have more of their claims covered. Another loser was Manville's Chairman McKinney, whose common stockholdings plummeted $189,000 in value. Manville's board, to the consternation of its creditors and shareholders, granted McKinney a $1.3 million retirement package.

Common Stockholders and the Reorganization

A week after Manville filed for bankruptcy in 1982 the stock price fell to a low of $5. In August 1984 the common stock was selling at $9 a share. Investors who purchased the stock at $5 the week after the company filed for bankruptcy would have earned a return on average over two years of 80%, or 40% a year. But for the old shareholders who had purchased the stock prior to bankruptcy filing during the heydays, Chapter 11 and the subsequent reorganization meant receiving as little as 2% of their original holding.

From August 1982 to August 1984 Manville's building materials and forest product businesses walked while competitors ran through one of the country's strongest economic recoveries. Its stock price plummeted from its prefiling days, although investors purchasing the stock after filing did well. Its marketing clout and long-standing commercial ties were seriously eroded. It spent $25 million and a lot of energy putting together a complicated reorganization plan. The unknown factor in the plan it proposed in August 1984 was the stock's potential. The company's sales and earning had been eroding since 1980 with negative earnings in 1982. One reason for Manville's poor performance was the erosion of its customer base after it filed for Chapter 11. Some customers believed that Manville had been disloyal and only cared about minimizing its own liability in the asbestos cases.

By August 1984 Manville had gotten rid of most of its asbestos product lines and had begun to deal with what creditors described as out-of-line overhead costs. Some of the cost problems were inherited from former CEO Richard Goodwin, who moved Manville to its fortress-like headquarters outside Denver and had a penchant for expensive acquisition. During the years since filing, Manville had become more of a law firm than a building products manufacturer. The company sued the federal government in six separate suits, claiming that the government carried a substantial responsibility to asbestos victims. This case was one they were destined not to win.

By July 1986 Manville's stock was trading at $3 a share. This was a 55 percent decline from 12 months earlier and a 200 percent decline from 24 months earlier. To have earned abnormal returns, it now appears, an investor needed to have purchased Manville's stock at the time of its filing and sold it by August 1984. Or an investor could have purchased the stock at its low of $3 a share and sold it at a price of $8 two years later in 1988. It is important to note that at one point during Manville's reorganization process its stock sold at $11. It appears that the final reorganization plan restricted that buying and selling of the stock as well as its growth potential to such a degree that the stock value may be undervalued. Manville's stock had shown an unusual level of volatility due to the market perception of a reasonably healthy company with a large uncertainty regarding its ultimate product liability. (A more recent example of a similar stock performance is that of Union Carbide with its associated Bhopal gas leak liability.)

A Price Mystery in Manville Stock

As required by the reorganization plan, new securities were issued to fund the trusts set up to benefit people injured by asbestos. Holders of old Manville common stock were to get one new share for each eight old shares they own. It is reasonable, therefore, to expect the old shares to trade at a price one-eighth that of the new shares.

Manville's old common stock closed March 31, 1989, in New York Stock Exchange trading at $2.50, while the new common traded at $7.625.

If the old common is reasonably priced then the new common should be worth $20.00; alternatively, if the new common is correctly priced then the old common should be trading at 95 cents. Why is the old common stock so overpriced, trading at more than two and one-half times its "fair" value?

Some possible theories are offered to explain this anomaly: (1) The possibility of a short squeeze. A trader who had shorted (borrowed and sold) eight shares of the expensive ("rich") old common stock and used the proceeds to buy the "cheap" new common stock stands to make a profit of $12.375, if the relative prices get back in line. To realize the profit one must be able to maintain the short position until the prices adjust. If the person who loaned the old common stock demands it be returned before that happens then the short seller may be forced back into the market to buy old shares to repay the loan. Some of these short-sellers would find themselves squeezed (hence, a short squeeze) by having to buy back the stock at a price higher than at which they shorted it. This would account for the relatively higher price of the old common. (2) The more uncharitable explanation is the unscrupulous broker theory. It holds that retail investors are buying the old shares in hopes of a bankruptcy turnaround, not understanding how the reorganization will dilute their stake, and that their brokers are failing to inform them of this outcome.

The other securities of the old Manville, ranging from preferred stocks to bonds, are trading in line with the prices of the new securities holders will receive in the reorganization. Holders of Manville's old bonds, who are big winners in the reorganization, have a choice of two packages of cash and securities, and the bonds are trading in line with the package that will produce the largest return. That package includes new preferred shares (March 31, 1989, NYSE closing price: $10.00) and fewer bonds than the other one.

TEXACO, INC.

On January 6, 1984, Texaco acquired Getty Oil. On the day after the deal Pennzoil filed a $14 billion lawsuit against Texaco for stealing Getty from it. At the time of the Texaco-Getty merger, Texaco agreed to indemnify Getty from any lawsuit filed by Pennzoil because of its failed attempt at merging with Getty. An interesting side line to the case is that Pennzoil's net worth was only about $1.2 billion at the time it sued Texaco.

The Megasuit

After years of battling in U.S. courts the case finally reached the U.S. Supreme Court in 1987. In April of that year the top court decided that

Texaco did indeed have to pay Pennzoil the $10 billion that a lower court jury had awarded Pennzoil, immediately. During the three-year legal battle Texaco's stock had dropped while Pennzoil's rose as speculators bet on the outcome of the court battle. It appeared that Pennzoil was in a better position than it would have been if the merger with Getty had been consummated. Pennzoil attorney Joseph Jamail, Jr. was even in a better position as his fee, if Texaco paid, would be $2.4 billion.

On the day in December 1985 when the jury awarded the $10 billion to Pennzoil, Texaco's stock dropped $3 to $36.25 while Pennzoil's shot up $7.62 to $57.50. Some 6.51 million Texaco common shares changed hands as speculators bought and institutional investors dumped the stock as its perceived risk rose. Two weeks later Texaco's stock had dropped to $25 a share. Moody's Bond rating service downgraded Texaco's bonds to BA1.

Pennzoil argued that even if Texaco had to borrow all $10 billion in cash it would only have a debt-to-equity ratio of 64% and that was a lot less debt than was carried by many other companies that had been through restructuring programs. At the time Texaco purchased Getty, Texaco's exploration cost for oil and gas was more than $26 a barrel—one of the highest in the industry. If one included the proceeds Texaco received from selling Getty's non-oil assets, one would discover it paid about $5.70 a barrel for Getty's domestic reserves.

If Texaco was forced to pay the entire $15 billion that Pennzoil had originally sought in actual and punitive damages, then the total cost of this oil would rise only to $12.25 a barrel. Texaco, on the other hand, argued that the real price difference between what Texaco paid for Getty and what Pennzoil offered was only $500 million. Unfortunately, Texaco's management argued for this cap on any award to Pennzoil after the jury had delivered its verdict. Whether an ordinary jury could understand the complex financial and legal issues of the case was questionable, as Texaco was forced into bankruptcy by its award to Pennzoil.

Texaco's Only Alternative: Filing for Bankruptcy

The $10 billion judgment was four times the total amount of money Pennzoil made in its 75 years of existence. It is 80 times the largest civil judgment ever paid in the United States, and 10 times the total net worth of Pennzoil.

In April 1987, after the final U.S. Supreme Court ruling against it, Texaco became the largest U.S. firm to ever seek protection from its creditors under Chapter 11 of the 1978 National Bankruptcy Law. Texaco tried frantically to settle with Pennzoil. After 17 months of intricate legal maneuvers since the 1985 award, the battle came down to a test of strength and nerve between resolute executives at two powerful corporations. Pennzoil's combative chairman, J. Hugh Liedtke, who stayed on past retirement to fight the case, refused to settle with Texaco for less than $3 billion. Texaco offered $500 million. Texaco essentially called Pennzoil's bluff and filed for Chapter 11.

Implications of Chapter 11 for Pennzoil

Under Chapter 11 Texaco was allowed to continue normal business operations. Its cash flow could improve as it would still receive revenue and did not have to pay interest payments on is $9.1 billion of debts. On the negative side Texaco could lose a great deal of business while under Chapter 11. Jobs of its 52,000 employees could be threatened. It would be forbidden to buy major oil assets without the approval of Texaco's creditors or a judge.

With Texaco in Chapter 11 Pennzoil stood to be a loser as well. Instead of having a priority claim to Texaco's assets, the smaller company would have to get in line with all the other creditors. Any payment to Pennzoil would not only be delayed, but might be for less than $10 billion. The threat of Pennzoil's claim became less immediate. Pennzoil could not attach liens to any Texaco property without approval of the court-appointed trustee. Pennzoil would still be able to collect any final judgment, but the Chapter 11 proceeding would force it to wait longer for its money. Another advantage of the Chapter 11 filing for Texaco is that it can set aside over $1 billion a year in cash by not paying dividends or interest on its unsecured debt. Interest on the amount it owes to Pennzoil also stops accruing—another $1 billion saved.

What was the stock management's reaction to Texaco's bankruptcy? On the day Texaco filed, the market dumped Texaco's stock and thus drove down the price. By the end of the day the price had risen to the level it was before the bankruptcy announcement, even though the company suspended dividend payments. Even Standard and Poor's promised to keep Texaco on its list of 500 leading stocks.

Many analysts believed that by filing for Chapter 11 Texaco had gained the upper hand in its battle with Pennzoil. Pennzoil shares, which had surged from $79.75 to $92.50 during the week before Texaco filing, plunged by more than 15 points the day after the Chapter 11 action and closed the week at $78. The Big Board seemed to judge that Pennzoil's chairman had overreached himself in the dispute. It had dragged on since November 1985, when the jury first issued the $10 billion judgment against Texaco. The bankruptcy action also would keep out of Pennzoil's grasp $3.6 billion of annual cash flow earned by Texaco's subsidiaries. Only Texaco's principal holding company and two financial subsidiaries are covered by the Chapter 11 filing. Dozens of operating subsidiaries around the world carried on business as usual. Pennzoil was surprised by this wrinkle in the bankruptcy law. Its management had thought that suing Texaco meant that all of Texaco was being sued. On Texaco's part, by not including its subsidiaries in the bankruptcy filing it kept the door open to more negotiations with Pennzoil.

Return on Texaco's Securities

For those interested in an investment in Texaco, some analysts at the time felt that bonds would be the best option. In June 1987 analysts figured that the common stock of Texaco could jump from $37 to $50, a gain of 35%, if the dispute with Pennzoil was settled by year end. Bondholders would get an even higher return, some 62%.

By December 1987 Texaco and Pennzoil had reached a settlement. Texaco agreed to pay Pennzoil $3 billion. The primary reason the two companies finally settled was that Carl Icahn, the chairman of TWA and an active corporate investor, had become the largest shareholder of Texaco and owned 12.3% of the common stock. He helped bring about the settlement, knowing that if the two companies settled the value of his shares in Texaco would rise. The settlement removed the uncertainty that had hovered over Texaco and enabled it to emerge from bankruptcy. By May 1988 Texaco's stock was at $50 a share.

Since Texaco's stock was selling at about $31 a share in April 1987 when the company filed for bankruptcy, investors purchasing the stock at that time and holding it until reorganization would have earned $19 a share or a return of 61%. The stock has continued to rise, closing at $53.60 on April 12, 1989.

MASSEY-FERGUSON COMPANY OF CANADA LTD.

Financial Statements

The Massey-Ferguson Company is a Canadian manufacturer of agricultural machinery. For the year ended October 31, 1978, the firm's net income was a negative $262 million. An abbreviated balance sheet and income statement for the year ended October 31, 1979, are shown in Tables 7.3 and 7.4.

Probability of Bankruptcy

After reviewing these two financial statements an investor may feel that the firm appears to be solvent and not in any danger. The current assets are larger than the current liabilities. Earnings are nonnegative. The equity of the firm is equal to the value of preferred stock plus the value of common stock and retained earnings. This value is equal to $578 million. The long-term debt of the firm is $658 million. Therefore,

Table 7.3
Massey-Ferguson Company of Canada Ltd., Income Statement for Year Ended October 31, 1979 (in thousands of dollars)

Revenues [a]	$3,125,000
Expenses (except interest)	$2,930,000
Interest expense	$164,000
Tax credit	$6,000
Net Income	$37,000

(a) Revenues include an extraordinary item of over $95 million, without which net income would be negative.

Source: Based on problem 5, chapter 31 of Weston and Copeland (1986).

Table 7.4
Massey-Ferguson Company of Canada Ltd., Consolidated Balance Sheet as of October 31, 1979 (in thousands of dollars)

Assets		Liabilities	
Current Assets	$1,935,000	Current Liabilities	$1,509,000
Other Assets	$810,000	Long-term Debt	$658,000
		Preferred Stock	$96,000
		Common Stock [a]	$177,000
		Retained Earnings	$305,000
Total Assets	$2,745,000	Total Liabilities and Shareholder's Equity	$2,745,000

(a) 18,250,000 shares with an average stock price in 1979 of $11.

Source: Weston and Copeland (1986).

the ratio of debt to equity is 1.14, which implies that the company is highly leveraged. An investor would not know if Massey-Ferguson is carrying too much debt until the average debt-to-equity ratio of the entire industry and that of the company cash flow statement are reviewed. The cash flow statement would indicate that the firm had enough cash to pay for its operational expenses and its interest expenses.

One way to predict if Massey-Ferguson may file for bankruptcy protection in the future is to apply a bankruptcy prediction model to the company (see chapter 6, section on "Financial Analysis and the Bankrupt Firm"). This model was developed by Altman (1968). To use the model the following five ratios from the company's financial statements need to be calculated:

1. Working Capital to Total Assets
2. Retained Earnings to Total Assets
3. Earnings Before Interest and Taxes to Total Assets
4. Market Value of Equity to Book Value of Equity
5. Sales to Total Assets

These ratios are then used in the following equation to obtain a number called the Altman Z score:

$$Z = 0.012 \times (\text{Working Capital to Total Assets}) + 0.014 \times (\text{Retained Earnings to Total Assets}) + 0.033 \times (\text{Earnings Before Interest and Taxes to Total Assets}) + 0.006 \times (\text{Market Value of Equity to Book Value of Debt}) + 0.999 \times (\text{Sales to Total Assets})$$

If the Z score is less than 2.675 then there is a large probability that the company will go bankrupt. If the score is above 2.675 then there is a large probability that the company will remain solvent. If one calculates the above ratios for Massey-Ferguson and uses the Z score equation, it appears very likely that the company will go bankrupt.

1. Working Capital to Total Assets $= (1,935 - 1,509) \div 2,745 = 15.5\%$
2. Retained Earnings to Total Assets $= 305 \div 2,745 = 11.1\%$
3. Earnings Before Taxes and Interest to Total Assets $= 195 \div 2,745 = 7.1\%$
4. Market Value of Equity to Book Value of Debt $= (18.250 \times 11) \div 2,167 = 9.3\%$
5. Sales to Total Assets $= 3,125 \div 2,745 = 1.14$ times
   $Z = 0.012\ (15.5) + 0.014\ (11.1) + 0.033\ (7.1) + 0.006\ (9.3) + 0.999\ (1.14)$
   $= 1.77$

Since 1.77 is less than 2.675, there is a high probability that Massey-Ferguson will go bankrupt in the near future.

Bankruptcy-Related Costs

Bankruptcy can mean that a firm incurs both direct and indirect costs. Direct costs include fees to professionals such as accountants and lawyers.[3] Indirect costs include the lost sales or profits due to the constraints imposed by the court or the court-appointed trustee. Altman (1984, p. 1087) estimated that for a sample of 19 industrial firms that went bankrupt, "bankruptcy costs ranged from 11 percent to 17 percent of firm value up to three years *prior* to bankruptcy." If management could observe early warning signals of bankruptcy, then these costs could be reduced by management arranging a merger with another firm or adopting a corporate reorganization plan at a more propitious time.

In 1980 Massey-Ferguson was on the point of financial collapse. The firm had manufacturing operations in more than 31 countries. Foreign debt obligations were owed by Massey's subsidiaries to local lenders of the countries where Massey had its operations. (These debts were denominated in the local currency.) On September 9, 1980, the company defaulted on all of its debt obligations. Prior to the time the company defaulted, it was incurring opportunity costs resulting from its position of financial distress. Some of these costs were:

1. Higher interest rates on new debt.
2. Increases in the time management spent in monitoring the firm's increasing debt position.
3. Loss of sales due to a weakened assurance of delivery.
4. An increasing inability to undertake otherwise profitable future investment opportunities.
5. An increasing probability of costly violations of the debts' restrictive indenture provisions.

Massey-Ferguson was also faced with an additional cost. Creditors began to demand that the firm be liquidated and the proceeds used to pay off claims. Liquidation of the firm would have resulted in large economic losses to society as well as the firm, its employees, and the suppliers because of the size of the firm and the scope of its operations.

Indicators of Financial Distress

There are several indicators of, or information sources about, the likelihood of financial distress that would have informed Massey-Ferguson's investors that the company was entering financial difficulty. One source is cash flow analysis for the current and future periods. A benefit of using this information source is that it focuses directly on the notion of financial distress for the period of interest. The estimates of cash flow included in this analysis are critically dependent, however, on the assumptions underlying the preparation of the budget.

A second source of information about financial distress is a corporate, competitive strategy analysis. This analysis considers the potential competitors of the firm or institution, its relative cost structure, plant expansions in the industry, the ability of firms to pass along cost increases, the quality of management, and so on. Ideally, these considerations also will underlie the cash flow analysis. However, a separate focus on strategy issues can highlight the consequences of sudden changes occurring in an industry. For example, in Massey-Ferguson's case an examination of break-even points and cost structures of its customers, who were mainly farmers, could have provided insight into which of its customers would be in financial difficulty should there be a dramatic drop in the demand for agricultural products.

A third source of information about financial distress is an industry-related analysis of the financial statement of the firm and those of a similar firm. In Massey-Ferguson's case an investor could have looked at the financial statements of another firm in the farm equipment industry, like John Deere. An investor could have also analyzed the trend in Massey-Ferguson's security returns over the past few years (refer to chapter 6, section on "Stock Market Analysis and the Bankrupt Firm") and also what rating its bonds were given by rating agencies such as Standard and Poor's or Moody's Investment Services.

NOTES

1. This background information was taken from "MCorp under Seige," a report published by Craig Davis and Randall Wooster for R. D. Smith & Company, Inc., December 15, 1988.

2. *The Wall Street Journal,* March 16, 1989.

3. According to the chief operating officer of Eastern Airlines, which filed for bankruptcy on March 9, 1989, simply filing in bankruptcy court would cost about $20 million in fees. *The Wall Street Journal,* March 8, 1989.

Bibliography

Aharony, J., C. P. Jones, and I. Swary. "An Analysis of Risk and Return Characteristics of Corporate Bankruptcy Using Capital Market Data." *The Journal of Finance,* Vol. 35, no. 4, September 1980, pp. 1001–1016.

Altman, E. I. "Financial Ratios, Discriminant Analysis and the Prediction of Corporate Bankruptcy." *Journal of Finance,* Vol. 23, September 1968, pp. 589–609.

———. "Bankrupt Firms' Equity Securities as an Investment Alternative." *Financial Analysts Journal,* Vol. 25, July–August 1969a, pp. 129–133.

———. "Corporate Bankruptcy Potential, Stockholder Returns and Share Valuation." *Journal of Finance,* Vol. 24, December 1969b, pp. 887–900.

———. *Corporate Bankruptcy in America.* Lexington, Mass.: Heath Lexington Books, 1971.

———. *The Financial Handbook.* New York: John Wiley, 1981, pp. 35.3–35.47.

———. "Discussion on Behavior of Firms in Financial Distress." *Journal of Finance,* Vol. 38, May 1983b, pp. 517–522.

———. *Corporate Financial Distress: A Complete Guide to Predicting, Avoiding, and Dealing with Bankruptcy.* New York: John Wiley, 1983a.

———. "A Further Empirical Investigation of the Bankruptcy Cost Question." *Journal of Finance,* Vol. 39, no. 4, September 1984, pp. 1067–1090.

———. "The Anatomy Of The High-Yield Bond Market." *Financial Analysts Journal,* July–August 1987, pp. 12–25.

———. "Measuring Corporate Bond Mortality and Performance." Working Paper, New York University, July 1988.

———. "Should We Regulate Junk Bonds?" *Financial Analysts Journal,* January–February 1989, pp. 8–9.

Altman, E. I. and M. Brenner. "Information Effects and Stock Market Response to Signs of Firm Deterioration." *Journal of Finance and Quantitative Analysis,* Vol. 16, 1981, pp. 35–51.

Altman, E. I., R. Haldeman, and P. Narayanan. "Zeta Analysis, A New Model to Identify Bankruptcy Risk of Corporations." *Journal of Banking and Finance,* June 1977, pp. 29–54.

Altman, E. I. and Scott A. Nammacher. "The Default Rate Experience on High-Yield Corporate Debt." *Financial Analysts Journal,* July–August 1985, pp. 25–41.

———. *Investing in Junk Bonds.* New York: John Wiley, 1987.

Arbel, A., S. Carvell, and P. Strebel. "Giraffes, Institutions, and Neglected Firms." *Financial Analysts Journal,* May–June 1983, pp. 57–63.

Argenti, J. *Corporate Collapse: The Causes and Symptoms.* London: McGraw-Hill, 1976.

Asquith, P. and E. Kim. "The Impact of Merger Bids on the Participating Firms' Security Holders." *Journal of Finance,* Vol. 37, December 1982, pp. 1209–1228.

Banz, R. W. "The Relationship Between Return and Market Value of Common Stocks." *Journal of Financial Economics,* Vol. 9, March 1981, pp. 5–18.

Bar-Yosef S. and L. D. Brown. "A Reexamination of Stock Splits Using Moving Betas." *The Journal of Finance,* Vol. 32, September 1977, 1069–1080.

Baskin, E. and G. Crooch. "Historical Rates of Return on Investments in Flat Bonds." *Financial Analyst Journal,* Vol. 24, November–December 1968, pp. 95–97.

Basu S. "The Relationship Between Earnings Yield, Market Value, and Return for NYSE Common Stocks: Further Evidence." *Journal of Financial Economics,* June 1983, pp. 129–156.

Beaver, W. H., "Alternative Accounting Measures as Predictors of Failures." *The Accounting Review,* January 1968a, pp. 113–122.

———. "Market Prices, Financial Ratios, and the Prediction of Failure." *Journal of Accounting Research,* Autumn 1968b, pp. 179–192.

Bernstein, P. W. "Who Buys Corporate Losers." *Fortune,* January 26, 1981, p. 60.

Black, F. "Capital Market Equilibrium with Restricted Borrowing." *Journal of Business,* Vol. 45, July 1972, pp. 444–455.

Black, F., M. C. Jensen, and M. Schole. "The Capital Asset Pricing Model: Some Empirical Tests." Reprinted in *Studies in the Theory of Capital Markets,* ed. M. C. Jensen. New York: Praeger, 1972, pp. 79–124.

Blume, M. and I. Friend. "A New Look at the Capital Asset Pricing Model" *Journal of Finance,* Vol. 29, March 1973, pp. 19–34.

Blume, M. E. and Donald B. Keim. "Risk and Return Characteristics of Low-Grade Bonds, 1977–1987." Rodney White Center for Financial Research, The Wharton School, University of Pennsylvania, Philadelphia, 1989.

Bodie, Zvi. "Common Stocks as a Hedge Against Inflation." *The Journal of Finance,* May 1976, pp. 459–470.

Box, G.E.P. and G. M. Jenkins. *Time Series Analysis, Forecasting and Control.* San Francisco: Holden Day, 1970.

Box, G.E.P. and G. C. Tiao. "Intervention Analysis with Applications to Economic and Environmental Problems." *Journal of the American Statistical Association,* Vol. 70, March 1975, pp. 70–79.

Breeden, D. "An Intertemporal Asset Pricing Model with Stochastic Consumption and Investment Opportunities." *Journal of Financial Economics,* September 1979, Vol. 7, pp. 265–296.

Breeden, D. "Consumption Risk in Futures Markets." *The Journal of Finance,* May 1980, Vol. 35, no. 2, pp. 503–520.

Brown, K. C., L. J. Lockwood, and S. C. Lummer. "An Examination of Event Dependency and Structural Change in Security Pricing Models." *Journal of Financial and Quantitative Analysis,* Vol. 20, no. 3, September 1985, pp. 315–334.

Brown, S. J. and J. B. Warner. "Measuring Security Price Performance." *Journal of Financial Economics,* Vol. 8, September 1980, pp. 205–258.

"Business Bankruptcies Soar." *Dun's Business Monthly,* April 1982, p. 29.

Calkins, F. "Corporate Reorganization Under Chapter X: A Post-Mortem." *Journal of Finance,* Vol. 3, June 1948, pp. 19–28.

Casey, C., V. E. McGee, and C. P. Stickney. "Discriminating Between Reorganized and Liquidated Firms in Bankruptcy." *Accounting Review,* April 1986, pp. 249–262.

Clark, T. A. and M. I. Weinstein. "The Behavior of the Common Stock of Bankrupt Firms." *The Journal of Finance,* Vol. 38, no. 2, May 1983, pp. 489–504.

Copeland, Thomas E. and J. Fred Weston. *Financial Theory and Corporate Policy.* 2d ed. Reading, Mass.: Addison-Wesley, 1983.

Corotto, A. F. and I. H. Picard. "Business Reorganization Under the Bankruptcy Reform Act of 1978—A New Approach to Investor Protections and the Role of the SEC." *DePaul Law Review,* Vol. 28, Summer 1979, pp. 961–1006.

Cox D. R. and H. D. Miller. *The Theory of Stochastic Processes.* London: Methuen.

Deakin, E. B. "Accounting Reports, Policy Intervention and the Behavior of Securities Returns." *The Accounting Review,* Vol. 51, July 1976, pp. 590–603.

Dewing, A. *Corporation Finance.* New York: Ronald Press, 1931.

Dimson, E., "Risk Measurement When Shares are Subject to Infrequent Trading," *Journal of Financial Economics,* Vol. 7, 1979, pp. 197–226.

Doherty, E. J. "Betting on Bankruptcies." *Financial World,* November 15, 1983, p. 47.

Economic Report of the President. Washington, D.C.: U.S. Government Printing Office, 1983.

Failure Record. Dun and Bradstreet, 1987.

Fama, Eugene F. "Efficient Capital Markets: A Review of Theory and Empirical Work." *The Journal of Finance,* May 1970, pp. 383–417.

———. *Foundations of Finance.* New York: Basic Books, 1976.

———. "Stock Returns, Real Activity, Inflation, and Money. *American Economic Review,* September 1981, pp. 545–564.

Fama, E. F., L. Fisher, M. C. Jensen, and R. Roll. "The Adjustment of Stock

Prices to New Information." *International Economic Review.* Vol. 10, February 1969, pp. 1–21.

Fama, E. and J. McBeth. "Risk Return and Equilibrium: Empirical Tests," *Journal of Political Economy,* May–June 1973, pp. 607–636.

Feller W. *An Introduction to Probability Theory and its Applications.* Vol. 2. New York: John Wiley, 1966.

Fischer, L. and J. H. Lorie. "Rates of Return on Investments in Common Stock— The Year-by-Year Record, 1926–1965." *Journal of Business,* Vol. 41, July 1968, pp. 291–316.

Fons, Jerome S. "The Default Premium and Corporate Bond Experience." *The Journal of Finance,* Vol. 42, no. 1, March 1987.

Golbe, D. L. "The Effects of Imminent Bankruptcy on Stockholder Risk Preferences and Behavior." *Bell Journal of Economics,* Vol. 12, Spring 1981, pp. 321–328.

Goldman Sachs Economic Research, *Financial Market Perspectives,* January 1989.

Gordon, M. J. *The Investment, Financing, and Valuation of the Corporation.* Homewood, Ill.: Richard D. Irwin, 1962.

Gordon, M. J. "Towards a Theory of Financial Distress." *Journal of Finance.* Vol. 26, May 1971, pp. 347–356.

Graham, B., D. L. Dodd, and S. Cottle. *Security Analysis, Principles and Techniques.* 4th ed., New York: McGraw-Hill, 1962.

Greene, R. and A. Bernstein. "Congratulations You're Bankrupt." *Forbes,* March 15, 1982, p. 114.

Grossman, Sanford and R. Shiller. "The Determinants of Variability of Stock Market Prices." *American Economic Review,* Vol. 71, no. 2, May 1981, pp. 222–227.

Hanna, M. "Corporate Bankruptcy Potential, Stockholder Returns and Share Valuation: Comment." *Journal of Finance,* Vol. 27, June 1972, pp. 711–717.

Haugen, R. and L. Senbet. "The Insignificance of Bankruptcy Costs to the Theory of Optimal Capital Structure." *Journal of Finance,* Vol. 34, May 1978, pp. 383–394.

Hershman, A. "The Big Bankruptcy Scare." *Dun's Business Month,* September 1982, p. 32.

Hickman, W. B. *Corporate Bond Quality and Investor Experience.* Princeton, N.J: Princeton University Press, 1958.

Hillmer, S. C. and P. L. Yu. "The Market Speed of Adjustment to New Information." *Journal of Financial Economics,* Vol. 7, 1979, pp. 321–345.

Hong, S. C., "A Bankruptcy Outcome: Model and Empirical Test." Working paper, University of California at Berkeley, March 1983.

"How to Profit When Firms Go Bust." *Dun's Business Monthly,* September 1982, p. 37.

Ibbotson, R. G. "Price Performance of Common Stock New Issues." *Journal of Financial Economics,* Vol. 2, 1975, pp. 235–272.

Ibbotson, R. G. and J. F. Jaffe. "Hot Issues Markets." *Journal of Finance,* Vol. 30, September 1974, pp. 1027–1042.

Ibbotson, R. G. and R. A. Sinquefield. *Stocks, Bonds, Bills and Inflation: His-*

torical Returns (1926–1978). Charlottesville, Va.: The Financial Analysts Research Foundation, 1979.

Jensen, M. C. "Capital Markets: Theory and Evidence." *The Bell Journal of Economics and Management Science*, Autumn 1972, pp. 257–398.

Jorgensen, D. W. "Econometric Studies of Investment Behavior: A Survey." *Journal of Economic Literature*, December 1971, 9, pp. 1111–1147.

Kendrick, J. W. *Productivity Trends in the U.S.* NBER Study. Princeton, N.J.: Princeton University Press, 1961.

Kendrick, J. W. and E. S. Grossman. *Productivity in the U.S.: Trends and Cycles*. Baltimore: Johns Hopkins University Press, 1980.

King, B. F. "Market and Industry Factors in Stock Price Behavior." *Journal of Business*, Vol. 39, 1960, pp. 139–190.

Larcker, D. F., L. A. Gordon, and G. E. Pinches. "Testing for Market Efficiency: A Comparison of the Cumulative Average Residual Methodology and Intervention Analysis." *Journal of Financial and Quantitative Analysis*, Vol. 15, June 1980, pp. 267–287.

Lintner, J. "The Valuation of Risk Assets and the Selection of Risky Investments in Stock Portfolios and Capital Budgets." *Review of Economics and Statistics*, Vol. 47, 1965, pp. 13–37.

Lintner, J. and R. Glauber. "Higgledy, Piggledy, Growth in America." Unpublished paper presented to the *Seminar on the Analysis of Security Prices*, May 1967, University of Chicago.

"List of Public Firms Which Have Filed for Chapter 11 Since October 1, 1979." Washington, D.C.: *Securities and Exchange Commission*, December 1982.

Livingston, M., "Industry Movements of Common Stocks." *Journal of Finance*, Vol. 32, 1977, pp. 861–874.

LoPucki, L. M., "The Debtor in Full Control—Systems Failure under Chapter 11 of the Bankruptcy Code." *American Bankruptcy Law Journal*, Vol. 57, 1983, pp. 99–126.

Markowitz, H. *Portfolio Selection: Efficient Diversification of Investments*. New York: John Wiley, 1959.

McClave, James T. and P. George Benson. *Statistics for Business and Economics*. San Francisco: Dellen Publishing, 1982.

McDonald, J. G. and A. K. Fisher. "New-Issue Stock Price Behavior." *Journal of Finance*, Vol. 27, March 1972, pp. 97–102.

McFadden, D., "Conditional Logit Analysis of Qualitative Choice Behavior." In *Frontiers of Econometrics*. ed. P. Zarembka. San Diego: Academic Press, 1974.

Meckling, William H. "Financial Markets, Default, and Bankrupt: The Role of the State." *Law and Contemporary Problems*, Vol. 41, Autumn 1977, pp. 13–38.

Meyers, Stephen L. "A Re-examination of Market and Industry Factors in Stock Price Behavior." *Journal of Finance*, Vol. 28, 1973, pp. 695–705.

Miller, M. and F. Modigliani. "Dividend Policy, Growth, and the Valuation of Shares." *Journal of Business*, Vol. 34, 1966, pp.411–433.

Miller, M. H. "The Wealth Transfers of Bankruptcy: Some Illustrative Examples." *Law and Contemporary Problems*, Vol. 41, Autumn 1977, pp. 39–46.

Miller, M. H. and M. Scholes. "Rates of Return in Relation to Risk: A Re-examination of Some Recent Findings." In *Studies in the Theory of Capital Markets*. ed. M. C. Jensen. New York: Praeger, 1972, pp. 47–78.

Moeller, Susan E. "Chapter 11 Filings: Good News for Investors?" *AAII Journal* (The American Association of Individual Investors), April 1986, pp. 9–12.

Moody's Manuals: Industrials; Banks and Finance; and OTC Industrials. New York: Moody's Investors Service, several issues.

Moore, John. "Foreword for Sessions on Economics and Bankruptcy Reform." *Law and Contemporary Problems*, Vol. 41, Autumn 1977, pp. 1–12.

Morgan Stanley. "Investment Perspectives." April 18, 1989.

Morse, Dale and Wayne Shaw. "Investing in Bankrupt Firms." *The Journal of Finance*, Vol. 43, no. 5, December 1988, pp. 1193–1206.

Perry, Kevin J. and Robert A. Taggart. "The Growing Role of Junk Bonds in Corporate Finance." *The Journal of Applied Corporate Finance*, Vol. 1, Spring 1988, reprinted in the *Financial Management Collection*, Vol. 3, no. 3, Fall 1988.

Pindyck, R. S. and D. L. Rubinfeld. *Econometric Models and Economic Forecasts*. New York: McGraw-Hill, 1981.

Ramaswami, M. "Stock Market Perception of Industrial Firm Bankruptcy." *The Financial Review*. Vol. 22, no. 2, May 1987.

Reilly, F. K. "New Issues Revisited." *Financial Management*, Vol. 6, Winter 1977, pp. 28–42.

Reilly, F. K., and E. Drzyciemski. "Alternative Industry Performance and Risk." *Journal of Financial and Quantitative Analysis*, Vol. 9, 1974, pp. 423–446.

Reinganum, M. R. "Misspecification of Capital Asset Pricing." *Journal of Financial Economics*, Vol. 8, March 1981, pp. 19–26.

Roll, R. "A Critique of the Asset Pricing Theory's Tests." *Journal of Financial Economics*, Vol. 4, March 1977, pp. 129–176.

Salomon Brothers. "The Anatomy of a Leveraged Buyout," by Brian Doyle and Hoyt Ammidon. January 1988.

Salomon Brothers. "High-Yield Corporate Bonds: An Asset Class For The Allocation Decision," by Paul H. Ross et al. February 1989.

Sanger, Gary. *Stock Exchange Listings, Firm Value and Market Efficiency*. Ann Arbor, Mich.: UMI Research Press, 1982.

Schnepper, Jeff A. *The New Bankruptcy Law*. Reading, Mass.: Addison-Wesley, 1981.

Schuchman, Philip. "Theory and Reality in Bankruptcy: The Spherical Chicken." *Law and Contemporary Problems*, Vol. 41, Autumn 1977, pp. 66–106.

Sharpe, William F. "Capital Asset Prices: A Theory of Market Equilibrium Under Conditions of Risk." *Journal of Finance*, Vol. 19, 1964, pp. 425–442.

Siegel, Sidney. *Nonparametric Statistics*. New York: McGraw-Hill, 1956.

Solomon, Ezra. *The Theory of Financial Management*. New York: Columbia University Press, 1963, pp. 55–68.

Stiglitz, J. E. "Some Aspects of the Pure Theory of Corporate Finance: Bankruptcies and Take-Overs." *Bell Journal of Economics and Management Science*, Autumn 1972, pp. 458–482.

Sunder, S. "Relationship between Accounting Changes and Stock Prices: Problems of Measurement and Some Empirical Evidence," *Empirical Research in Accounting: Selected Studies,* 1973, pp. 1–45.

Trost, Ronald J. "Corporate Bankruptcy Reorganizations: For the Benefit of Creditors or Stockholders?" *U.C.L.A. Review,* Vol. 21, 1973, pp. 540–75.

Warner, J. "Bankruptcy, Absolute Priority, and the Pricing of Risky Debt Claims." *Journal of Financial Economics,* Vol. 4, May 1977a, pp. 239–276.

Warner, J. "Bankruptcy Costs: Some Evidence," *Journal of Finance,* Vol. 33, May 1977b, pp. 337–347.

Westerfield, R. "The Assessment of Market Risk and Corporate Failure." Working Paper, Wharton School of Finance, August 1970.

Weston, F. J. "Some Economic Fundamentals for an Analysis of Bankruptcy." *Law and Contemporary Problems,* Vol. 41, Autumn 1977, pp. 47–65.

Weston, F. J. and Thomas E. Copeland. *Managerial Finance.* 8th ed. Chicago: The Dryden Press, 1986.

White, M., "Economics of Bankruptcy: Liquidation and Reorganization." Working Paper, New York University, August 1981.

White, M. "Bankruptcy Costs and the New Bankruptcy Code." *Journal of Finance,* Vol. 38, May 1983, pp. 477–488.

White, M., "Bankruptcy Liquidation and Reorganization." In *Handbook of Modern Finance,* ed. D. Logue. Boston: Warren, Gorham and Lamont, 1984.

Wichern, D. W. and Jones R. H. "Assessing the Impact of Market Disturbances Using Intervention Analysis." *Management Science,* Vol. 14, November 1977, pp. 329–337.

Index

ABOUT THE AUTHORS

MURALI RAMASWAMI is a Senior Vice President and Director of Product Development at the Travelers Investment Management Company (TIMCO) in Hartford. He received Ph.D. and M.A. degrees from Boston University and an M.B.A. from the Indian Institute of Management, Ahmedabad. Prior to joining TIMCO, Dr. Ramaswami was an Assistant Professor of Finance at Northeastern University, Boston. He has also taught at Boston University and done research at the Harvard Business School. He was employed as a senior economist by Data Resources, Inc., Lexington, Massachusetts, and worked on the input output macroeconomic model of the U.S. economy. As a project director with the Institute for Development Research in Boston, Dr. Ramaswami has extensive experience in consulting with international government agencies and public enterprises. He was also employed as an economic analysis officer by Exxon, India (ESSO). He has published extensively in the areas of microeconomics of industrial organization, corporate bankruptcy, futures and options, and global finance and is a frequent speaker at industry and academic seminars.

SUSAN E. MOELLER is an Assistant Professor of Finance at the University of Michigan in Flint. She received her B.S., M.B.A., and Ph.D. degrees from Michigan State University. She was employed as a product planning analyst by Ford Motor Company, coordinating product engineering, cost, and profitability objectives for advanced vehicle programs. Dr. Moeller has also taught at Northeastern University in Boston. She has published extensively in the areas of corporate bankruptcy and international finance.